'For those fighting the pressure to turn schools into factories and young people into products, this book is timely, pertinent and radical. It offers an alternative perspective on education, one that resonates strongly with those of us passionate about democracy, participation and inclusion. It is not a dry academic textbook but is exciting and refreshing. More than this, it is a call to action.'

Dr Max A. Hope, Centre for Educational Studies, University of Hull

'Coffield and Williamson are to be congratulated on providing a very accessible, succinct and practical account of the current socially destructive trends in education policy based on...neo-liberalism, and how policy change might be organised from the standpoint of educators in the field. A particular strength lies in the way the authors demonstrate how their notion of means of gaining consensus for makes a positive contribution

Dr Helen Raduntz,
Education, Equity and ..., University of South Australia

'This succinct booklet makes compelling and thought-provoking reading. The style of writing generates a sense of urgency culminating in a spine-tingling call for action in the names of both professional liberty and social justice for learners. Coffield and Williamson argue passionately for a radical shift away from dominant political discourses based on targets and the market-value of education. Instead, they challenge readers to think differently about the nature of education and present a plan for generating collaborative "communities of discovery" that have the potential to overcome the constraints of the present system. The book is both timely and topical, focusing on some of the most pressing issues in contemporary UK society. It will no doubt stimulate much-needed debate. By unsettling the status quo, Coffield and Williamson strengthen the moral imperative to act now in order to rescue the future of education in the UK. Readers are left in no doubt that there is no time to delay.'

Dr Caroline Sarojini Hart, University of Cambridge

'This book is a passionate plea for making education in schools, colleges and universities more meaningful and more democratic. Frank Coffield and Bill Williamson not only show where things went wrong, but also provide concrete suggestions for how we might put them right. A must-read for anyone who believes in the power of education.'

Gert Biesta, Professor of Education, University of Stirling, Scotland

'Frank Coffield and Bill Williamson share their powerful vision of democratic educational communities to replace the profoundly flawed system we have now in the UK, USA and countries around the world. Grounded in a deep knowledge of education politics, a passionate commitment to democracy, and the moral urgency to act now, this concise book provides change-makers with the inspiration to build the kinds of communities that are the foundation for a more just and sustainable society.'

Dana Bennis, Director of Research and Programs at IDEA, the Institute for Democratic Education in America

'From Exam Factories to Communities of Discovery extends Professor Frank Coffield's seminal work, Just suppose teaching and learning became the first priority.... Teachers and trainers, as well as others with a passion for learning that is driven by curiosity and collaboration, will find the case for an education whose aim is to tackle the biggest questions and dangers of our time irresistible. "Communities of discovery" give a means for creating such an education system and engaging practitioners. Are we beyond needing a clarion call to shut up factories for exams and skills and transform them? Frank and Bill find not, and sweep from the panoramic to the particular of our times to excite, pepper and persuade, stripping back policy architecture in order to get to the heart of "what is the aim of education". Readers are invited and inspired to take action, so that as educators we create an "educational spring" and awakening where learning is the central organising principle.'

Toni Fazaeli, Chief Executive, Institute for Learning

From Exam Factories to Communities of Discovery

The Bedford Way Papers Series

A full list of Bedford Way Papers, including earlier books in the series, can be requested by emailing ioepublications@ioe.ac.uk

From Exam Factories to Communities of Discovery
Discovery
The democratic route

Frank Coffield and Bill Williamson

Institute of Education, University of London
Bedford Way Papers

First published in 2011 by the Institute of Education,
University of London, 20 Bedford Way, London WC1H 0AL

www.ioe.ac.uk/publications

British Library Cataloguing in Publication Data:
A catalogue record for this publication is available from the
British Library

ISBN 978 0 85473 917 2

Typeset by Quadrant Infotech (India) Pvt Ltd
Printed by ImageData Group

Contents

List of abbreviations

A level	Academic examination usually taken by students in England at the age of 18
DBIS	Department for Business, Innovation and Skills
ESRC	Economic and Social Research Council
FE	further education
GCSE	General Certificate of Secondary Education, an academic examination usually taken by students in England at the age of 16
HE	higher education
NEET	Not in education, employment or training
NIACE	National Institute for Adult and Continuing Education
OECD	Organisation for Economic Co-operation and Development
Ofsted	Office for Standards in Education
plc	public limited company
ULC	Union Learning Representatives

Acknowledgements

In writing this book we used our notion of a **community of discovery** by getting a close circle of friends to test out, sharpen and extend our ideas. So we are most grateful for the time and effort expended by John Bynner, Emma Coffield, Tony Edwards, John Lowe, Iain Rodger and Paul Wakeling. Tony Edwards also produced a Preface that neatly summarises our approach.

We are also indebted to the five reviewers chosen by the Institute of Education, who encouraged us, for example, to see democratic education in a more international light. Mary Coffield then neatly turned our succession of messy drafts into a publishable text. Finally, we want to thank Jim Collins, Nicole Edmondson, Sally Sigmund, Michele Greenbank, Yvonne Percival and Martin Hargreaves for the care and attention to detail they have shown in the production of this book.

29 June 2011

Preface

When the incoming New Labour Government proclaimed a commitment to 'standards not structures', it was announcing a radical shift in priorities from organisation (usually on market principles) to 'high quality education for the many rather than excellence for the few'. Since 1997, however, structures have been rearranged, again and again. The outcomes described in this book have been a system unfit for its own declared purposes, and damagingly narrow in what it is intended to achieve.

Frank Coffield and Bill Williamson begin by deploring what has become the natural language of policy-making, the language of targets to be reached and products to be delivered. They offer instead very different ways of thinking about learning, and of how examination 'factories' might be transformed into 'communities of discovery'. By doing so, they recognise their vulnerability to being dismissed as faint voices from a 'progressive' educational establishment, properly drowned out in the new world of entrepreneurs, brand-makers and managers. So they not only describe the dire effects of successive directives from above; but they also provide a clear, passionate account of how different the 'system' could be if the mutually supportive relationships of teachers and learners became the focus of thinking about education. Their main theme is the replacement of top-down reforms with enforced routes 'from policy to practice' by truly democratic practices both where learning takes place and where its conditions are planned and arranged.

This is not an academic analysis for fellow academics, or even for current policy-makers, who are very unlikely to be persuaded. There are references to evidence, and to other constructive heretics against market and managerial orthodoxies, but the authors are writing for learners of all kinds and for those who work with them. What they themselves stand for is never in doubt, and controlled anger at how things are develops into a passionate vision of how they might be.

Tony Edwards
Emeritus Professor of Education
University of Newcastle upon Tyne

About the authors

Frank Coffield is Emeritus Professor of Education at the Institute of Education, University of London (IOE). He previously worked at the universities of Newcastle, Durham and Keele; at Jordanhill College of Education; an approved school; and a comprehensive school in Glasgow. He was director of the ESRC's programme of research into *The Learning Society* from 1996 to 2002. His first book was on Glasgow gangs and his most recent publications, all downloadable free of charge from the website of the Learning & Skills Network (LSN), are: *Just suppose teaching and learning became the first priority...*; *All you ever wanted to know about learning and teaching but were to cool to ask*; and *Yes, but what has Semmelweis to do with my professional development as a tutor?*. He has recently been awarded an honorary doctorate by the University of Bedfordshire.

Bill Williamson is Emeritus Professor of Continuing Education at Durham University. He is married with two grown-up children and six grandchildren whose futures worry him deeply. They tease him about his being a sociologist who is always fretting about the state of the world. He tells them that a career as a sociologist in higher education (in Newcastle and Durham), doing research on education and on many aspects of social change, showed him there is much to fret about! He explains his concern at the contrast between the social mobility (but lower living standards) of his generation and the lack of it (despite higher living standards) for the younger generation today. He wrote about this in *The Temper of the Times: British society since World War Two* (Blackwell, 1990). His grandchildren complain to him about school. They find school boring. He tells them, based on his experience as Director of Continuing Education at Durham University and his research on lifelong learning (e.g. *Lifeworlds and Learning: Essays in the theory, philosophy and practice of lifelong learning* (NIACE, 1998)), that they should not despair. They will continue their education at work and throughout their lives. Research and consultancy over the past decade working on projects about both socially excluded people and the further professional development of well-qualified people in work, convinced him of the liberating power of learning and the inextricable link between learning and creativity described in his (with Bob

Garvey) *Beyond Knowledge Management: Dialogue, creativity and the corporate curriculum* (Pearson, 2003). He hopes his grandchildren believe him when he explains that they are not trapped; they can make changes to their lives and to their world. It takes knowledge, commitment and creative work with others, but it can be done.

Chapter 1

Breaking the consensus on education

'That's the trouble with words. You never know whose mouth they were in last'.

Dennis Potter[1]

Introduction

A book on the power of democracy to transform education must be written in democratic language, accessible to all. So we begin with a promise to our readers: we shall not use any jargon, we shall present our arguments in clear English, and if we occasionally use a technical term, we will explain it in a note. As we are not writing primarily for our academic colleagues, we will not pepper our text with references to the academic literature; however, we do need to acknowledge our considerable debts to other writers and thinkers by mentioning them in the text, with fuller details in notes at the end of each chapter and a full bibliography at the end of the book.

We have written this book for the benefit of educators working in a wide variety of settings – in schools, colleges and universities, in work-based learning and within communities – and for all those who despair that the current educational policies of the three main political parties in England (and similar ones elsewhere) are set to continue. We reject their policies, because the summit of their ambition is to reform, yet again and in different ways, the present 'system'. That 'system', however, is deeply undemocratic, inequitable, inefficient and inadequate to address our present problems and future threats. That 'system' does not need to be reformed – it needs to be replaced.

To use an analogy from the transport industry, it is as if all our policies in education are like the efforts of road hauliers to make their old-fashioned juggernauts travel faster on modern, overcrowded motorways. They can make as many marginal adjustments to fuel injectors, transmissions and exhaust systems as they like, but they remain trapped within the logic of a transport system that is essentially absurd. Improvements in the design of juggernauts only amplify congestion and increase environmental damage. Such marginal improvements in the technology of the juggernaut highlight the absurdity of vehicles invented in the early twentieth century struggling to cope on twenty-first-century motorways. Similarly, in education the response of politicians and policy-makers to any difficulty has always been to build an extension to the 'system' (e.g. pupil referral units were created to deal with disruptive behaviour) rather than to deal with the underlying causes of the difficulty. In this way, a grotesque educational juggernaut has been pieced together and added to over the years and is now a shuddering pantechnicon, some parts of which are nevertheless capable of excellent performance.

Despite many different viewpoints, the main political parties and the ever-increasing number of think tanks, advisers, education journalists, teachers' unions, employers' associations, worried parents and pressure groups that frame the key debates on education have this one aim in common: they want change within current, taken-for-granted assumptions about the purposes of education. They want to keep making changes so that our 'system' catches up with, and then overtakes, those judged the best in the world. They all appear to accept the simplistic belief that a 'world-class' education 'system' will automatically improve the competitiveness of our economy and so ensure that prosperity keeps on growing, at least for those in secure employment.

There is, however (to push the transport metaphor harder), thick fog ahead on the motorway along which this juggernaut is trundling, but it is now being forced to increase speed without a clear view of the dangers in front of it. The many drivers on board are all pulling different levers to improve its performance, with only a vague notion of where it is headed: a society of aspiration and opportunity. This is a laudable ambition until the fog lifts and suddenly there is a pile-up ahead, and no one knows what has caused it or how to remove it or how to stop the juggernaut in time. We need to act before the old juggernaut crashes into the back of the queue of cars ahead.

Reclaiming the language of education

We also need to care more about the effects of language on our educational thinking and practices. We should abandon such arrogant phrases as *'future proofed'* (have we learned nothing from the financial crisis of 2008?); *'seamless progression'*, especially when the 'system' loses thousands of learners at transition points; and *'UK plc'*, the phrase from *'managementspeak'* that reduces the diversity, richness and vitality of British society to the narrow concerns of a public limited company. Politicians of all parties also talk about *'raising standards'*, but by this term they mean nothing more than raising the test scores of students in a limited number of subjects. We need to return to more collegial forms of address; for example, *'head of department'* rather than *'line manager'*, as there are no production lines in education, only ways of treating educators as if they were *'producers'* of standard *'products'*. Schools, colleges and universities have become *'providers of learning opportunities'*, and quality in education has come to mean conforming to government policy, as enforced by Ofsted, the inspection service.

We place so much importance on this point because in the last 30 years the language of management and economics has virtually replaced the language of education. The process is insidious: at first hearing, such phrases as *'the bottom line'*, *'the business model'* and *'more for less'* are clearly limited and objectionable, but within a short time, so great is the power of money, that we catch ourselves using them without a qualm.

Junk language is as damaging to our minds as junk food is to our bodies; it corrupts our thinking but it also dehumanises our relationships. Performance management has turned students into *'customers'*, then into *'inputs and outputs'* and finally into the contemptuous phrase *'bums on seats'*. This phrase concentrates on one part of a student's anatomy – but not on the place where psychologists have located the seat of learning. For years now, managers have been unashamedly talking about *'bums on seats'*; slick publishers produce books with patronising titles about how to get the *'buggers'* to behave,[2] but educators should insist on respect for all their students.

For some years now, some educational institutions have, under pressure from the market, moved beyond mere advertising to marketing themselves as brands in order to develop their 'business'. They employ full-time brand managers with branding assistants (to wield the branding iron, no doubt), whose job it is to produce brand value and brand visual identity, brand guidelines and brand templates, a brand book and 'signoff protocols for externally facing literature'. (These are real examples taken from a university's marketing strategy.) A strategic marketing group is then established, with the 'mission' of training 'faculty champions', producing 'customer relationship management solutions' and conducting 'competitor analysis' in order 'to create a culturally impactful presence'. Such 'brand development' will apparently enhance corporate strategy by 'extending global reach' (this means attracting a few more foreign students who will pay top fees). Resources of money, time and energy are spent on branding and rebranding – resources which could have been used to prevent job losses, to train staff or to attend to the needs of students. Educational institutions are diminished, rather than enhanced, by their trite brand images.

We do not mean to imply that senior staff voluntarily choose to develop such marketing strategies. Rather, faced with the prospects of intensifying competition from academies and 'free' schools which may result in further cuts, closures or redundancies, managers feel compelled to adopt such market mechanisms as branding in order to seek advantage over competitors. In this way, they too are being dragged under the wheels of the juggernaut, which turns school against school, college against college and university against university.

We agree with Gert Biesta that 'the language of education has largely been replaced by a language of learning'.[3] Teaching, he argues, has been reduced to facilitating learning, education has been reduced to the provision of learning opportunities, and adult education has come to mean nothing more than employability skills. 'Employability' is an ugly word for the ugly idea that learners should willingly accept the responsibility of constantly updating their skills in the hope that an employer will one day recognise their constant struggle to remain fit for employment by offering them a job, any job. So the term 'lifelong learning', which retains some liberating and democratic possibilities, is increasingly being used as an instrument of control. Politicians and employers insist that it is up to learners to keep themselves up to date and, if they are unemployed or made redundant, they have only themselves to blame because they have not learned enough. The trick being played here is simple but highly effective, because the language of lifelong learning transfers responsibility away from ministers and employers to individuals.

We want to argue in reply that the focus of public attention should not be on individuals, but on the structure of opportunities. The problems are not demotivated young people or work-shy adults. The vast majority of people want to work as much as they ever did. The problems are the lack of decent jobs and the lack of progression and training in the low-paid jobs that do exist. In the UK in 2011 there are almost a million unemployed 16 to 25-year-olds. Chief executives in both the private and public sectors have seized the opportunity of free labour by exploiting young people who are desperate to work by offering unpaid internships, while paying themselves mega-salaries, bonuses and pensions.

At the same time, young people disengage from school in their hundreds of thousands, as they have been doing for generations. For decades, they have been claiming that the curriculum is irrelevant to their needs, interests and futures, but successive governments have turned a deaf ear to this inconvenient message. Once they have left school, the only choices open to these young people are the same as they were in the 1980s, when they described them as: 'shit jobs, govvie schemes or the dole'.[4]

Young people continue to disengage in significant numbers because they feel that the schooling on offer does not meet their needs. They are not wrong in this, and they are seriously disadvantaged by the assumption that too many are left to make: namely that prolonging their education is not in their long-term interests. There are complex cultural factors at work that explain the poverty of expectations of many working-class young people. Formal schooling of the kind that has been offered to them did not, and does not, offer them challenging or engaging options. Alison Wolf's recommendation that those who fail to obtain a C grade at GCSE English or Maths should continue taking exams until they pass, is likely to result in further disengagement.[5]

Since 1988, Conservative, New Labour and the Conservative-led Coalition governments have claimed that we need a national curriculum to establish a basic entitlement for all students and so raise standards across the board. Let us accept these two claims at face value for the moment. Even so, shouldn't a national curriculum also be relevant to the present and future lives of those who have to study it? For years, John White, the English philosopher of education, has repeatedly stressed that, when we are designing or redesigning a national curriculum, it would be sensible to start by agreeing on its aims: 'This means working out first of all what the curriculum is meant to be for; and only after that deciding what vehicles are best to take us to our destinations'.[6] The hard task of deciding on the aims of education is being avoided by the Coalition Government, as it has been by all its predecessors; and the clapped-out juggernaut of our educational 'system' is not up to the task of taking us where we need to go. We require, first and foremost, a genuinely open, public debate about the content and purposes of education and how it can renew our society.

We will use the term 'education' as the overarching idea within which the more limited term 'learning' is located. To us, education is the dynamic combination of such elements as:

- the transaction between the generations where historians or chemists or beauticians show students how to think and act like historians or chemists or beauticians by introducing them to the knowledge, skills and understandings of these disciplines;
- the means of creating the kind of society we want by opening minds, transforming lives and civilising society;
- a critical understanding of society by encouraging independent thinking and collective action;
- a commitment to improving the learning of all;
- a simultaneous matching of society to the needs of learners and of learners to the anticipated and debated future needs of society;
- the preparation of all citizens as full, active members of a democratic society.

For the sake of variety we will refer to both 'learners' and 'students', but will talk about 'educators' rather than 'teachers' or 'tutors' to emphasise both the broad, liberating remit of education and all the valuable learning that takes place outside schools and colleges. For us, the process of education is much more than an economic transaction, in which education is reduced to the status of a commodity that is 'delivered' by the 'providers' – the teachers – in order to meet the needs of the 'consumers' – the students – with these needs defined by the 'providers'. It is also much more than the dry, technical business of transmitting information to students, a process for which the pejorative term 'schooling' is more appropriate.

Some readers may ask: what is so wrong with treating our students as consumers or clients? If the customers are king, they may very well refuse the 'product' on offer. Government policy papers argue on the one hand that assessment should become more rigorous and, on the other, that students should be treated as customers. But how are educators to tell these 'customers' that they will fail if they do not submit their assignments on time or if their work is not up to the required standard? The relationship between educators and students must be such that the former can assess the work of the latter (and even fail some of their assignments) without that relationship breaking down. Teaching is not only complex intellectually, it draws on all our emotions – it is a subtle art to criticise students and still keep them motivated to improve.

Let us give a more specific example from post-compulsory learning and training. It is dispiriting to discover that, after 11 years of compulsory schooling, the following are the highest demands that some young people make of the staff: the right to smoke anywhere in college, the need for sufficient parking places directly in front of the building where they have classes, and the provision of nothing but burgers and chips in the college canteen. Is it our role as educators just to fulfil these desires? The analogy with businesses such as British Telecom or British Gas satisfying the needs of their customers is seductive but false, because it ignores the role of educators who, at times, have to stand up to students, coax them out of their 'comfort zones' and challenge them to try disconcerting ideas and new ways of looking at themselves. If we, as educators, are there simply to respond to the self-proclaimed needs of students, then what are we to do when students ask, as a few have done in the past, for coursework that does not involve them in any sustained work? Or when students who have been tested and retested every year since they started school want you to tell them the one book, or better still, the one article that will ensure them an A grade? Many students are attracted into education precisely because they do not know what their needs are. Our proposals cannot be dismissed as the fuzzy, soft outpourings of two white-haired lefties (well, we plead guilty to the latter charge), but rather should be seen as the rigorous and hard-headed reflections from two working lives within education, from our knowledge of the research literature and from shared reflections with other educators on practice.

There is, however, another language used to discuss education, which is just as alienating as that of management, and that is the language of much of the social sciences. We shall follow the charitable practice of the Roman Emperor Marcus Aurelius, who, in his *Meditations*, never failed to record the names of those of whom he approved, but who drew a discreet veil of secrecy over those he thought had behaved badly. Who, for example, is likely to be inspired to take action by such terms as 'conscientisation' or 'legitimate peripheral participation' or 'transgressive holism' or 'prefigurative practice' or 'transcendental violence' or 'pedagogisation', which is difficult even to pronounce? The literature on education and lifelong learning is disfigured by such terms, but, more importantly, potential supporters are turned off. Our own particular pet hate is 'co-construction'. Can you imagine educators and students marching on Whitehall chanting the inflammatory words – 'What do we want? Co-construction! When do we want it? Now!' These clumsy terms are used to lend a spurious complexity to ideas that are essentially simple; for what does 'co-construction' mean but to build together?[7] Some of the worst damage is done to education not by its enemies, but by its jargon-ridden friends.

Social scientists who use such ugly neologisms seem to have forgotten Karl Marx's famous insight: 'The philosophers have only interpreted the world differently; the point is to change it'.[8] We would caricature the outcome of the inelegant use of language by some social scientists as follows: If you describe the world in such off-putting terms, no one will still be reading when you come to make recommendations about how to change it.

What questions should we be asking?

The most important debate to have about education is this: how can we help more people to engage in creative forms of new learning that will enable them to overcome not only the deep-seated, cumulative obstacles of inequality faced by the many, but also the collective threats now faced by us all?

In the short-run, the spending constraints, imposed by the Coalition Government on the public services to deal with the economic crisis created by the financial sector, will further restrict the possibilities for change in education throughout the UK. Nevertheless, within those constraints there are choices to be made. Those choices on offer at the moment by the Coalition Government on the right and by New Labour on the left of political life in England, and by the devolved administrations in Scotland and Wales, point to a future of acrimonious conflict, but conflict within the traditional terms of the debate. We must break out of this self-defeating consensus.

Nowhere is the cross-party consensus more clearly seen than in contemporary educational debates, where the parties seek to outdo one another in promoting educational excellence and opportunities, while their words speak of a view of society and of human possibility that is decidedly short term and instrumental. The politicians look superficially at a few aspects of a successful 'system', such as Finland's, and then draw naive, crude and misleading lessons for policy from the comparison. Tim Oates, Chair of the expert panel set up by the Secretary of State for Education in England to review the curriculum, has persuasively argued that for a 'system' to be regarded as coherent, at least 13 aspects (including content, assessment, inspection, the structure of institutions, funding, governance and selection) need to be 'aligned and reinforce one another'.[9] But for the last 30 years, ministers have tinkered with one aspect of the curriculum after another without considering the impact of, say, rigorous and repeated assessments on the motivation of students or the quality of their learning.

As we go to press, Tim Oates is quoted as saying that 'the curriculum has become narrowly instrumentalist'[10] and that climate change and other such topics may be dropped from the revised national curriculum. Instead we should concentrate, as the Secretary of State for Education in England puts it, on providing 'a world class curriculum that will help teachers, parents and children know what children should learn at what age'.[11] While we, too, believe strongly in the centrality of knowledge of science and other academic disciplines, we also remember A.N. Whitehead's admonition that: 'A merely well-informed man is the most useless bore on God's earth'.[12] We must move beyond the false distinction of using *either* tradition ('the comfort of the ostrich'[13]) *or* the application of knowledge to social problems as the main argument in deciding what we should teach. We urgently need knowledge from the physical and social sciences and the humanities to help us address the threats we face and, in the process, we will create new knowledge. There is, however, a logical inconsistency in Tim Oates' insistence, on the one hand, that, 'Teachers do not need to be told how to do their jobs'[14] and, on the other hand, the curriculum review panel, which he chairs, prescribing the core scientific knowledge that all students should learn.

In this book, we will use not a new vocabulary, but a different one, because we wish to challenge the taken-for-granted language of the current debate. We urge people who work in or talk about education to stop using the language of the market and start using words and phrases like: 'democracy', 'trust', 'collaborative learning', 'the courage to take risks' and 'creative discontent with current economic and environmental conditions'. Such words have the power to challenge a debate that relies on terms like 'targets', 'high stakes testing', 'efficiency', 'learning outcomes' and 'world-class' schools; and to challenge such bleak evocations of the power of language and the beauty of mathematics as in phrases like the 'literacy hour' and the 'numeracy hour', to distinguish them, no doubt, from the illiterate and innumerate hours that precede and follow them.

This sterile language of performance management carries no criticism of the world being built around us; it is designed to control professionals, it ignores the threats we face and has an atrophied sense of human possibility. The use of the word 'aspiration' by all three political parties is typical. Our politicians are agreed: education is about helping people to realise their aspirations. But our aspirations are shaped by our families and our class, and in our society they are also highly commercialised. So it is not surprising that people are motivated to want what this society or their family or friends expect them to achieve. The core aspiration is to become a financially successful, self-interested and dedicated consumer, not an engaged citizen in a democracy concerned with improving the well-being of all.

The language of democracy is not being spoken. The policies that would build wide, open-ended and free learning opportunities at all stages of life in order to give meaning to the term 'democratic education' are not even being considered. Instead, the dominant thrust in education debates is to improve the competitiveness of the British economy. Our concern is that other, equally important goals – the democratic, social and cultural purposes of education – are being quietly forgotten, because in modern societies economic arguments tend to trump all others.

There is also a worrying silence from our three political parties about the explosive growth of a highly skilled but low-wage workforce (in Asia and South America as well as in the West), which challenges the notion of any simple relationship between learning and earning. The conclusion of years of international comparisons by Phillip Brown, Hugh Lauder and David Ashton[15] is that the promise held out by governments to students – study hard, gain qualifications and you will land a good job with a comfortable lifestyle – has been broken by the fierce, global competition for the dwindling supply of middle-class jobs.

Overview of our approach

We give an overview of the main differences between the current market model of education and our more radical approach in Box 1.1 (overleaf), where we distinguish the workings of power at the three levels of: the system, the institution and the classroom. Such a list is neither exhaustive nor empirical, but it is descriptive. It is an aid to further reflection, debate, revision and action. For the present we want to give a flavour of our thinking. We want, for instance, to criticise explicitly those educational institutions that have come to resemble businesses rather than learning communities. Box 1.1 represents our desire to redress the baleful effects of the dominant rhetoric and to replace them with a new language and a new practice in education that express democratic possibilities.

Learning encourages the creativity and the risk-taking needed for change, as when citizens use their minds, exercise their human rights, treat others with respect and challenge the status quo. Such conditions develop when members of a group (a school, a company, a university, a local authority or a political party) assess the democratic credentials of their organisation, take a longer term view of the future they are working towards or seeking to guard against, and then to decide to work together for reform.

Box 1.1: Moving from the present model of education to our radical alternative

		THE MARKET MODEL $\longrightarrow$		COMMUNITIES OF DISCOVERY
SYSTEM LEVEL	1.	Government stress on performance management, targets, competition	1.	Emphasis on the democratic rights of enhancement, inclusion and participation
	2.	Regulation is punitive, disproportionate and poor value for money	2.	Self-regulation, moderated by peers, directed towards improvement
	3.	The learning environment is restrictive and only the 'core' staff are trained	3.	The learning environment is expansive and develops the abilities of all
	4.	The main driving force is fear	4.	The main driving force is trust
INSTITUTIONAL LEVEL	5.	Institutions are seen as the 'providers' of skills and qualifications	5.	Learning is the central organising principle of our institutions
	6.	All important learning takes place in formal settings	6.	Informal learning is prized as a vital form of learning
	7.	Dissent is treated as disloyalty to senior management	7.	Dissent is positively encouraged as a means of organisational learning
	8.	Teachers are seen as agents of government policy who teach what and how government tells them to	8.	Educators are professional, lifelong learners who improve their work for the sake of doing a better job
	9.	Students are seen as 'consumers' of 'products' who should be 'streamed' by ability	9.	Learners are citizen educators, all of whom are capable of improvement
CLASSROOM LEVEL	10.	Teaching seen as the transmission of skills and information from tutors to students, whose minds are 'empty buckets'	10.	Teaching and learning seen as one process, as two sides of one coin
	11.	Learning seen as the individual acquisition of knowledge, skills and qualifications	11.	Learning is collaborative; dialogue plays a central role, and helps create more equal power relations between educators and learners
	12.	Knowledge is capital to be turned into profit	12.	Knowledge is a collective resource

The two approaches presented in Box 1.1 are admittedly caricatures rather than accurate descriptions, set up deliberately in opposition to one another in order to emphasise their differences. Most administrators, politicians, managers and tutors would probably place themselves at different places along this continuum rather than at either end, although when you listen to certain ministers, not only in the UK, it is obvious that market principles are what matter most. Educators, for instance, are increasingly caught in the middle between, on the one hand, their professional commitment to their students, and, on the other, carrying out the business plan of their senior managers. They seek to reconcile these competing interests by adopting a broad spectrum of strategies: from appearing to comply, to shielding students from the effects of too much imposed change, to leaving the profession, if all else fails. There is, however, little outright resistance.[16]

Tensions can become acute if the financial interests of the school take precedence over the educational needs of the student, for example when a school offers a vocational option which it is not equipped to teach. The recent Wolf Report on vocational education referred to young people 'being deceived and placed on tracks without their full understanding and consent'.[17] So much for students being at the heart of the present 'system'.

In their turn, senior managers are like football managers with a board of directors/governors (and government ministers) on top of them and professional players/tutors below them; as a result, they end up severely stressed by pressures from both sides. The pressure from above comes from constant changes in policy and funding, and the pressure from below comes from educators who resent the constant surveillance and control. We need to move away from such a 'system', which relies largely on fear to effect change.

Our view of democracy and communities of discovery

The market model has turned our schools and universities into exam factories and our further education (FE) colleges into skills factories. The level of discontent with this state of affairs is rising among students, parents and educators, but that discontent is at present unfocused and uncoordinated. We propose both an alternative future – **communities of discovery** – and the means of getting there – by realising the collective creativity of students and educators through **democracy**. We need to explain what we mean by these terms that are the heart and soul of our argument.

We define **democracy** not just as a form of government, not just as the activity of voting in a secret ballot once every four years, not just as majority rule and the protection of the rights of the minority, but as **the most equitable and harmonious means of living, learning and working together**. A democratic education would encourage learners to form an image in their heads of the kind of society in which they want to live and how they can bring it into being.

We owe it to Amartya Sen and other writers to ensure that our thinking about democracy goes beyond European and American models; that it goes beyond balloting and majority rule to include public reasoning and 'the extent to which different voices from different sections of the people can actually be heard';[18] and the realisation that democratic institutions only work if people seize the opportunities to *practise* democracy within them.

This book is an unashamed polemic, an exercise in public reasoning, and an attempt to change the direction in which educational reform is headed. In more detail, we want to change the terms of the debate within education from an obsession with standards and skills to embrace a much more fundamental concern: the need to strengthen democracy. To achieve this, we must redistribute power within education and we shall do this by building **communities of discovery**. By this term we mean that within schools, colleges, universities, workplaces and civil society, **learners and educators must work together with democratic practices and values to discover new ways to address the main threats to our collective well-being.**

In 1991, Jean Lave and Etienne Wenger,[19] two American anthropologists, transformed the understanding of learning by shifting the focus of analysis from an individual absorbing information to participating in what they called 'communities of practice'. By that term they meant 'groups of people informally bound together by shared expertise and passion for a joint enterprise',[20] such as football supporters' clubs, political pressure groups and book clubs. This shift in attention stressed the essentially social character of learning, and we wish to acknowledge the intellectual debt we owe to both authors for 'locating learning squarely in the processes of participation, not in the heads of individuals'.[21] One of the many virtues of their fresh look at learning is that our attention is switched from the assimilation of information by individuals to the importance of access to learning and of the social arrangements and resources for learning.

We now wish to extend Lave and Wenger's 'communities of practice', which is unfortunately a rather dull and uninspiring term, but which rightly emphasises collaborative participation in groups as the best way of understanding learning. Instead, we want to popularise the term 'communities of discovery', a more colourful and inspirational phrase, to describe the creative engagement of citizen-learners at all stages of their lives in tackling the collective problems we face in new ways.

The issue that lies behind all the discussion so far is power. In communities of discovery, power is openly, widely and more equally shared among the members of those communities, whose main task is to encourage all citizens to play an active part in their democracy. In later chapters we will expand on our notion of communities of discovery and we will suggest how the current structures of power in education can be challenged to strengthen democracy. That will mean confronting the old elitist model, which still flourishes in our leading universities, as well as the business model that has taken over so many of our schools and colleges.

The private sector grows fat in an age of austerity

What drives our argument is the sense that, if we carry on as we are doing, the future will be bleak. Austerity is no short-term problem. The evidence from across the world points to an intensification of the competitive pressures of globalisation and, in the West, of continued efforts to reduce public spending on welfare. But the pressure being exerted by all three political parties in England for permanent reform of public services is a powerful part of the governing consensus that we wish to break. Of course, all public services, including health and education, could and should be improved, but the excessive concern with reforming them is diverting attention from the more pressing need to **reform the private sector** in case taxpayers' money has once more to be poured into the banks to save the financial sector from collapse.

Let us try to summarise what the future of education is likely to be if we continue with current policies. The maintained sector will face: an insistence that more must be done with less, as cuts bite deeply into all the public services; more educators being sacked, while ministers claim that front-line services are being supported; more diversity, choice and selection being introduced to protect and intensify existing hierarchies among institutions; repeated, wasteful structural changes; new initiatives being imposed on top of existing initiatives, none of which are evaluated; an ever-expanding list of new responsibilities for educators; pressure for ever higher test scores and different sets of qualifications, which will masquerade as higher standards of education; one funding formula being swiftly replaced by another; more privatisation and more public/private partnerships, as public funds are transferred to the private sector; requirements for intensified competition and increased cooperation to run simultaneously; sharply widening gaps between the attainments of students from advantaged and disadvantaged homes; more intrusive surveillance of professionals and more rigorous inspections of institutions; more millions being wasted on the inspection service, Ofsted, as it strives to prove we are getting value for money; and fear as the main driving force of change.

We predict: wave after wave of redundancies; a further lowering of morale among educators; intensifying disaffection among parents and learners; and a growing resistance from professional educators, which may result in strikes, even from headteachers, as they seek to defend their pensions and working conditions from government depredations.

Despite enormous political pressure to change – largely to save money to cut the public debt – resistance to the latest round of imposed changes will intensify. To return to the juggernaut analogy used earlier, marginal improvements to educational performance are proving ever harder to achieve. Cries from the business community that standards are falling will intensify, as will graduate unemployment and debt. Graduates are already taking jobs that do not require degree-level qualifications, when they can get jobs at all; and resentment will increase among non-graduates who face higher levels of unemployment because graduates are taking their jobs.

Such resentments will strengthen the electoral support of racist, right-wing parties that will encourage their supporters to believe that their disadvantages are a consequence of high levels of immigration. The elite universities will become even more socially exclusive, and middle-class parents will desert the urban comprehensives for the quieter, more socially exclusive pastures of the private schools, faith schools and 'free' schools. In short, the elitist model of superior education for the privileged will be protected and reinforced.

At the time of writing, the Government's White Paper on higher education, *Students at the Heart of the System*, has just been published with its commitment 'to opening up the higher education market, including to Further Education colleges and alternative providers'.[22] Its contents confirm our suspicions. Elite universities will be given additional places to be filled by students with the highest A-level qualifications, who come in the main from private schools. New types of provider will be allowed the title of 'university' to broaden out market-led opportunities for those who are less well qualified.

The first step is to stop and take stock, and to look ahead as far as we can and think about questions such as: Are the policies of the three main parties in England adequate responses to the problems we face? What are the problems for which our current arrangements for learning are the solution? Do they provide a basis for building the kind of society and global order we would wish to be part of in 30 years' time?

There are powerful forces at work in the modern world telling people how they should imagine their future lives. The worst excesses of the twentieth century were perpetrated by men and women who knew what they wanted the future to be and imposed their will on their societies. The madmen have not gone away. We have a new lot. As before, too many people are trapped in circumstances that leave them unable to challenge the ideas of those seeking the power to define their future.

As we see it, the challenge for educators is threefold. First, our work should be informed by an alternative vision of the future for the learners we guide. Second, we should take an informed, critical view of our own practices and of the institutions within which we work and should be willing, in concert with other like-minded professionals, to change both. Finally, we have a responsibility (though not exclusively) to build our work on an explicit and adequate diagnosis of the times we live in. To that task we turn in the next chapter.

Endnotes

1   A comment made by dramatist Dennis Potter in a TV interview shortly before he died in 1994.

2   There is a series of books with such titles as *Getting the Buggers to Behave* by Sue Cowley, 2010.

3   Biesta, 2005: 54.

4   A 'govvie scheme' is a government scheme to help young unemployed people and the 'dole' means unemployment benefit. The phrase was used by young people in the North East in a study by Frank Coffield, Carol Borrill and Sarah Marshall in 1986.

5   The Wolf Report on vocational education, 2011.

6   White, 2010: 2.

7   Coffield, forthcoming.

8   Quoted by Mills, 1963: 71.

9   Oates, 2010: 13.

10   Oates, as quoted in Shepherd, 2011b.

11   Gove, 2011.

12   Whitehead, 1962: 1.

13   Young, 1961: 73.

14   Oates, 2011.

15   Brown, Lauder and Ashton, 2011.

16   See Coffield *et al*, 2008, for a detailed discussion of the strategies adopted by tutors.

17   Wolf, 2011: 83.

18   Sen, 2009: xiii.

19   Lave and Wenger, 1991.

20   Wenger and Snyder, 2000: 139.

21   Hanks, 1991: 13.

22   DBIS, 2011: 10.

Chapter 2

A diagnosis of our time

'The wrong type of democratic education will tend to transform everything into terms of vocational training and adjustment to an industrial order'.

Karl Mannheim and Campbell Stewart[1]

Introduction

In the middle of the Second World War, Karl Mannheim published a *Diagnosis of Our Time*,[2] in which he reflected on how Europe could climb out of the disaster of totalitarianism. We want to follow Mannheim's suggestion that there is, implicit in everything we do, a 'diagnosis of our time'. Such diagnoses provide an interpretation of the ways in which a society is changing and the problems that it will need to face in the future. On the basis of these diagnoses, educators plan curricula and formulate ways of teaching and learning to help people learn how to overcome the obstacles that stand in the way of the future they desire.

In a pluralistic world, a large variety of futures will be envisaged. They range from prosperous, liberal democracies to theocracies of a most illiberal kind. In the recent past, the future was defined in totalitarian terms and millions of people were forced to live under the jackboot or the threat of incarceration in the Gulag. Millions continue to live in abject poverty, close to the limits of human survival. They learn daily that they are of no importance to anyone, that their lives are dispensable.

The history of formal education in this country can be read as the story of how different diagnoses of our times shaped educational provision so as to define, for each generation, the rationale for what they were expected to learn at school. For the Victorians it was the threat of social disorder that had to be met through a strict schooling of the working classes to learn the three 'Rs' and to respect the authority of their social 'superiors'. In the twentieth century, education changed gradually to meet the need for a better educated labour force for a changing economy. Today, educational policy is framed by a concern to promote international competitiveness and economic growth in a globalised economy. In each case, the political interests of the most powerful in society shaped, and continue to shape, the educational opportunities of the majority.

As we have noted, the dominant contemporary diagnosis of our time, which is shared by the main political parties, is remarkably uniform (with small differences of emphasis). It is that we must carry on building a society to reach a future in which everyone is prosperous and equipped with skills to help them compete for the rapidly diminishing number of 'decent' jobs – but there is a huge, internal contradiction here, as there are not enough professional/ managerial jobs available. It is just assumed that formal education at all levels must be aligned with the perceived needs of the economy. Differences among the political parties revolve more around the means of doing this than around the end itself. The demand for a better educated workforce and for people with a greater understanding of science and technology is viewed as an indispensable element of the 'grow-as-we-are ideology', with its naively optimistic belief that all our problems can be solved through current management techniques.

There is a myopic understanding of future threats to our society and of how people learn. At least two things need to change to improve the prospects of developing a framework of learning in the UK fit to meet the challenges of the future. First, we need to debate and then act upon a new 'diagnosis of our time'. Second, we need to challenge ourselves and all educators and learners – not just those in formal education – to help others to learn and to think creatively and critically. Since, as R.H. Tawney once pointed out, 'life is a swallow, theory is a snail',[3] this work must be undertaken continuously, for the dangers will keep changing.

The future cannot be known, but we must debate its possible shapes. There are those who look ahead and, like Sir Martin Rees,[4] calculate that the human race has only a 50 per cent chance of survival by 2050. Noam Chomsky[5] has likewise suggested that international economic competition, coupled with global warming, will exacerbate conflicts and, as long as nuclear annihilation remains a real threat, conceivably result in the extinction of humanity.

These dystopian nightmares are likely to be dismissed as exaggerated. Nevertheless, there is a built-in uncertainty and unpredictability to the outcomes of the actions both of individuals and organisations (including nation states and international bodies) that are unmanageable. A paradoxical feature of modern rationality is that, wherever it is applied, it results in unpredictable, new risks for which yet more new 'solutions' are needed. One consequence is that as the global interdependence of communities intensifies, the risks of conflict and catastrophe also increase, despite the best efforts of most societies to minimise both. Our ability to plan for a future we desire is therefore much less than we imagine it to be.

Challenging 'globespeak'

An important constraint on our ability to approach these questions critically is the language we use. The language of globalisation – let us call it 'globespeak' – dovetails well with that of managerialism and results in a valuation of human beings that is essentially utilitarian. People become valuable as 'human capital' or 'human resources', not as citizens with human rights who are capable of showing each other respect and understanding. They are encouraged to develop new skills to serve the purposes of others, not new ways of understanding themselves and changing their world.

We exaggerate, of course, but not much, and the exaggeration helps to identify this question: Does 'globespeak' provide us with the conceptual tools to secure a better future? We do not think so. At times of crisis we cannot afford to fall back on the managerial language and the policies that have failed and continue to fail.

The right of people to fulfilling work has degenerated across the globe into an employer-led demand for people to be given an education that will fit them for such jobs as are available. The logic of modern capitalism demands 'human capital', and governments across the world have attempted to meet this demand in the ways they provide for education and training. Critics of what is a neo-conservative agenda that is being pursued in many countries – in the USA, Australia, in East Asian countries like Singapore and, of course, in the UK – stress that a narrow focus on skills runs the risk of inhibiting creativity and a wide cultural awareness. Other critics claim that this approach devalues a broader, humane education for citizenship. Others question the logic of providing people with a narrow set of skills for jobs that do not yet exist, the skills for which are at present unknowable.

The case for tying education closely to the skills demands of employers seems compelling, at least at first sight. If people lack basic skills, they will find it hard to find decent jobs. It also remains the case that huge numbers of school leavers (and, therefore, over time, many adults) do lack a good command of the basic skills necessary for both employment and civic engagement. According to the Wolf Report, 'We are failing at least 350,000 of our 16–18 year olds, year by year'.[6] We are not against helping people to develop their abilities to work and lead fulfilled lives. These are aims we support, but we do not think they are being met within current arrangements for education and training.

Tadpole philosophy

Human beings are capable of much more than politicians and employers imagine. There are still educational dinosaurs like the recently knighted Chris Woodhead, a former Chief Inspector of Schools in England, who play a prominent role in defining the current neo-conservative approach to education policy, and who believe that there are natural hierarchies of academic ability. He is chair of a private company, Cognita, that runs independent schools. In an interview with *The Guardian*,[7] he argued that middle-class children had better genes and that some children were born 'not very bright'.

In 1931, at the height of the economic crisis and when a coalition government was cutting public services to rescue the ailing economy, R.H. Tawney called such thinking, the 'Tadpole Philosophy'. He put it this way:

> It is possible that intelligent tadpoles reconcile themselves to the inconveniences of their position, by reflecting that, though most of them will live and die as tadpoles and nothing more, the more fortunate of the species will one day shed their tails, distend their mouths and stomachs, hop nimbly on to dry land, and croak addresses to their former friends on the virtues by means of which tadpoles of character and capacity can rise to be frogs.[8]

The consolation of this philosophy, he explained, is the belief that exceptional individuals can succeed in overcoming the evils of their social disadvantage, but resentment is bound to build up among those tadpoles who do *not* reconcile themselves to remaining forever tadpoles. He knew that a seriously unequal society such as ours would always blight the opportunities of the many, while privileging those of the few.

Eighty years on, we know in much more detail the manner in which lives are not only limited but damaged, for example, through poor health, higher mortality rates and social inequalities.[9] Tadpole philosophy has not, however, gone away. It still carries the widely held, but false, belief about natural differences of ability and seeks to justify the view that education should be differentiated both in structure and curricula to reflect that. It follows for those who subscribe to such views that it is wrong to shoehorn those who are not academically gifted into courses in which they can never properly succeed.

Such thinking does not result in a plea for an inclusive education for all, of the sort that once inspired the idea of comprehensive education. It results in the development of socially divided schools and academic hierarchies. R.H. Tawney's message, however, remains relevant. He did not criticise inequality on the basis of a false belief that people are all equally endowed with ability and therefore should all have the same opportunities in education (or, we would add, the chance to develop personally and to continue learning in work and in civil society). On the contrary, like him, we would press the view that we should celebrate the differences that make people unique and that, as he put it, it is 'the mark of a civilized society to aim at eliminating such inequalities as have their source, not in individual difference, but in its own organisation'.[10]

People can be helped to develop a different story about their lives and to acquire a new sense of personal agency, which we think of as 'the ability to give direction to one's life.'[11] Pessimistic thinking of the sort exemplified by Chris Woodhead is immune to such ideas, and the policy-makers and educators who follow this approach end up in the mental cul-de-sac of incorrigible elitism.

Racial, gender and religious discrimination

Elite groups across the world have always liked to believe that their power, status and success, and therefore the social inferiority of those they dominate, are the outcome of natural inequalities of ability. Such beliefs have a long history and they extend far beyond the field of education. By doing so, they damage learning opportunities and limit the lives of millions. The history of the civil rights movement in the United States and of anti-colonial struggles across the world must in part be written around rejecting deeply held racist beliefs that black people were inferior in intelligence to white people. Yet this racist belief determined how people of colour have been schooled in white-dominated societies and how their failure to flourish in education was explained and continues to be explained.

That same struggle has left us with a legacy of ideas and practices about combating racism that we can build on. Through mass demonstrations, boycott campaigns, legal actions against discrimination, committed journalism, social research, all the way through to acts of personal courage to support those who have been humiliated, racist thinking was successfully exposed for the absurd nonsense that it is and discrimination made illegal. Racism has not been killed off and we must remain vigilant against it, but at least we now know how to deal with it.

There are obvious parallels in the continuing battle for gender equality. Beliefs about the innate, biologically determined differences between the sexes were once deployed to justify the socially and politically inferior status of women. It is a problem gradually being overcome in many western societies, but it remains entrenched in other parts of the world. Misogyny woven into the social institutions of society is endemic in the Middle East and in other parts of the Islamic world. By denying educational opportunities to women, such societies put a brake on their prospects for social and economic development and lend a spurious legitimacy to the political domination of the weak by the powerful. By doing so, they place severe limits on the political imagination of the oppressed. In deference to either tradition or to the false belief that their faith demands it, millions of women across the Muslim world – and elsewhere – collude in their own oppression.

At the same time, many are now rejecting traditional definitions of their roles. The so-called 'Arab Spring' or 'Arab Awakening', which is currently blossoming across the Middle East and in which millions of Arabs, communicating with one another through social networking sites, are demanding freedom from oppression, is a series of complex movements in which women – particularly young, educated women – are playing a prominent role. They are demanding equal rights to men and are determined, against the grain of the dominant political cultures, to play their role in the political life of their societies.

It would be wrong to assume that these problems are far away or that they will be overcome through economic development. It is a feature of the global economy that its metropolitan centres in the developed world are populated with significant ethnic and religious minorities. People from the developing world are living and working within the social fabric of the developed societies. France is home to over five million Muslims of North African origin and a similar number of Turkish origin live in Germany. Across Europe there are minority ethnic populations whose origins are in the Middle East, Africa and Asia.

Living democracy

The political issues raised by the presence of minority ethnic populations touch all aspects of our societies and severely test prevailing ideas about citizenship, human rights and intercultural understanding. People from different cultural backgrounds in our societies challenge ideas about what it means to be British or Spanish or European and, much more fundamentally, what it means to be a human being in a world where all our lives are increasingly interdependent.

There is in these observations a Gordian knot of racism, social disadvantage and political powerlessness to be cut open. It is a knot tightened by ignorance of other cultures, by narrowly drawn nationalism and by fears of being 'swamped' by strangers. Modern societies could become threatened by inter-ethnic violence and a general lack of faith in the capacity of democratic institutions to solve collective problems.

Those problems can no longer be confined within the boundaries of nation states. The education-for-employment model is blind to these kinds of issues. Globalisation pitches every society into an intense economic struggle to improve skills, productivity and competitiveness. The economy, however, is only one of the battlegrounds on which the future safety and well-being of modern, democratic societies rests. An exclusive focus on the economic aims of education devalues not only liberal values in learning, but also the idea of democracy that is at the centre of our societies. By so doing, it builds a very weak version of citizenship and one that is ill-suited to equip people with the knowledge and confidence to engage constructively with the public life of their societies.

Progressive educators across the developed world are aware of these ideas. In the United States, public intellectuals (such as Martha Nussbaum, Amy Gutmann and the English-educated Ghanaian philosopher Kwame Appiah[12]) have sustained a critical discussion about the intellectual, cultural and educational challenges faced by modern democracies. Social scientists like (to name but a few) the Indian intellectual Amartya Sen, the Spanish urban sociologist Manuel Castells, the American educator Michael Apple and the Hong Kong based David Grossman, Wing On Lee and Kerry Kennedy[13] have enriched our understanding of the threats to democracy in the modern world.

Of the many themes they have discussed, we believe there are four that stand out as not strongly represented in British political debates, where the role of education in strengthening democracy is very muted. *First,* the strong message from American progressives, with their intellectual roots in the philosophy of John Dewey, is that an education defined by economic goals is not only wrong in its neglect of the arts and humanities, it is also dangerous for democracy. It is not that a liberal arts education makes good democrats; it is that a good critical education, which enables people to think for themselves and to debate with others, to respect them and to engage with the political life of their societies and not merely their own local communities, is a necessary requirement of a healthy democracy.

What Amy Gutmann calls 'deliberative democracy'[14] requires people to acquire the knowledge and skills that will enable them to engage in critical discussion with fellow citizens. Without such debate, it is not possible for there to be what both she and Amartya Sen call 'public reasoning', so that the rationale behind public policies can be assessed and agreement about them secured through politics rather than authoritarian imposition. In a world where extremist views (about religion, politics, sexuality and science education) exist, and where there are profound moral disagreements between people, informed public reasoning is always under threat.

In her coruscating criticism of profit-driven education policies (in the USA, the UK and in India), Martha Nussbaum put the case this way:

> *I shall argue that cultivated capacities for critical thinking and reflection are crucial in keeping democracies alive and wide awake. The ability to think well about a wide range of cultures, groups, and nations in the context of the global economy and of the history of many national and group interactions is crucial in order to deal responsibly with the problems we currently face as members of an interdependent world.*[15]

Nussbaum is not against a strong and successful business culture (nor are we), but even this depends on what she calls 'a climate of watchful stewardship', creative innovation, and the same skills of dialogue and engagement that support democratic practice. We take from her the idea that democracy cannot be taught as if it were just another subject in the curriculum. It is an ideal to be lived in practice and which invites us to question whether our educational and social institutions are sufficiently open and tolerant to allow democratic practice to shape the public reasoning that should govern decisions about how we should live our lives.

Nor do we want to lose sight of the *second* theme: Nussbaum's insistence on how interdependent we have become and how the main dangers we face, such as climate change or nuclear accidents, call for collective action. Alan Wood, the American historian, wants the USA to move beyond the 1776 Declaration of Independence towards:

> *a new statement of principle – a kind of Declaration of **Inter-Dependence** – that realigns our national and global priorities to respond to our present array of challenges.*[16]

We do not wish to simplify too far or to generalise too freely, for the situation is complex. Across Europe, for example, as we learn from the work of Audrey Osler and Hugh Starkey,[17] educators are searching to find a means through their curricula to express the importance of ideals about European citizenship. There is a balance to be struck between respecting the strong regional, political identities which exist across the continent (as, for example, in Catalonia or Scotland) and endorsing general European values about justice, fairness, human rights and freedom, while recognising the dangers of splitting up into smaller groups in the fight over scarce resources. Besides, there are multiple and mutually supportive identities such as those who are passionate about, say, Welsh nationalism *and* the European Union.

The development of curricula inspired by European ideals is made difficult by the presence of diverse national, ethnic and religious identities. To seek to impose a common European frame around diverse cultural differences runs the risk of excluding some groups, especially Muslims, from the political life of the continent. Political extremists can and do exploit such dangers. Terrorist attacks on civilian targets in Madrid and London, by people born in Spain and in the UK respectively, are stark examples of those dangers, as are the routine acts of discrimination experienced by minority ethnic groups.

In an interdependent world, knowledge of the civic education of others is vital to an understanding of our shared international order and what threatens it. The threat from Islamic extremism in the period after the attack on the World Trade Center in New York in 2001 has altered a great deal of the politics of the modern world. The American educators Thomas Scott and John Cogan have noted the impact of 9/11:

> *The Bush education initiatives are consistent with the neo-conservative approach to civic education that, since September 11th has emphasised American patriotism, respect for the flag, the moral force of prayer, a Christian national identity and a messianic duty of the United States to transfer the benefits of democracy, free markets and American values around the world.*[18]

Scott and Cogan claim that teachers who are not in agreement with these principles do not speak out for fear of criticism from parents and civic leaders. Their main point, however, is that this version of citizenship education does not build the global perspective that people need in order to understand the world they live in.

Our *third* theme, which was well understood by Karl Mannheim in the early days of the Second World War, is that the defence of the overarching values that nurture democracy, and the dialogue that is at its heart, has to be maintained on a continuous basis. Mannheim noted that if we and our 'best thinkers' do not do it, 'there will be others less scrupulous'[19] who will do a very different kind of job. The form such defence must take is to ensure – but with no blueprint in mind, far less a master plan – that the institutions within which we work give expression to the central values of democracy that guarantee our dignity, our freedom and human rights and celebrate our social interdependence and solidarity as human beings.

Our *fourth* and final point here is that nobody knows how best to bring about the changes to our institutions that democracy demands. And the reason is clear: there is no one solution. There is no one model of 'good practice' on which to draw. As times change and new threats to democracy emerge, we have to think in innovative ways to overcome them. We have to discover together the changes we need to make – and these will vary from country to country and from locality to locality.

This challenge can only be met in collaboration with others who share a 'diagnosis of our time' and keep their understanding of it fresh. We can reflect on past efforts to refashion social arrangements and try to learn from them. But that is not enough. We have to make judgements about current arrangements and imagine other options.

As Kwame Appiah[20] did in his study of moral revolutions, those which swept away the institution of the duel, of foot binding in China, of slavery in the Americas, and which seek today to eradicate honour killing in Pakistan, we have to look forward to a time when our descendants will look back at us with astonishment and ask of our practice of democracy: 'What were they thinking?' If they do so with either a sense of shame or ridicule, we will have challenged successfully the lazy idea that what we do today is the best we are capable of.

The future in the past

During the Second World War, Lord Beveridge captured the imagination of the British people with a plan for social reconstruction once victory was secured.[21] He famously identified the five giants that must be slain to clear the road to social reconstruction: Ignorance, Disease, Squalor, Idleness and Want. Free education, public healthcare, full employment, decent housing and social security would clear them away. At the same time, Karl Mannheim highlighted the importance of building democratic systems of education to prevent civilisation imploding once again, as it had done in his country under Nazism. For Mannheim, democracy had to become '**militant**'[22] if it was to survive.

This was a widely shared view among liberal thinkers at the time. For example, in 1942, R.G. Collingwood, historian, archaeologist and philosopher, as his contribution to the war effort, argued that European civilisation faced the dangerous threat of 'barbarism'.[23] He was clear that existing educational institutions provided no defence against this threat. By the end of the war, the evidence of the consequences of barbarism in Europe was there for everyone to see in the Holocaust.

With hindsight, it is clear that Beveridge, Mannheim and Collingwood had all underestimated the changes needed to build a better society – one that respects human rights and achieves fairness, justice and security for all. The giants have not been slain. They have changed shape and regrouped, and new ones, such as inequality, have been identified as threats. Our case here is not that we should return to the analyses of the 1940s. We take from that period the understanding that **militant** democracy was the safest antidote to totalitarian violence. The three commentators judged their moment in history and the dangers imminent within it, and forged a way of thinking to overcome them. The dangers would not be met without profound change in social institutions and particularly in those that nurtured democratic ideals. Education was at the centre of their thinking, but their view of it was largely school- and university-based.

Despite a decade or more of citizenship education in schools and profound changes in international relations that have made the world a much more dangerous place, British people vote in elections with little enthusiasm. In 1983, 70 per cent of 18 to 24-year-olds voted in the general election. In 2005, the figure was 40 per cent and in 2010, 53 per cent. Membership of political parties is falling and there is widespread cynicism about politics and real anger about politicians who break their election pledges as soon as they gain power. The consensus among political scientists is that, without radical constitutional reform in Britain, this disengagement from politics will only get worse.[24]

Our claim is different. It is that the democratic institutions of this society – not only those of representative government – must be strengthened. A stronger model of democracy is needed to secure both human rights and the intellectual creativity needed to solve our collective problems. Democracy cannot be taught, it must be lived. To achieve that, we have to struggle for profound changes in the ways in which our educational institutions are structured, managed and experienced.

We, too, must have the intellectual courage to look back and to look forward, to assess the strengths and weaknesses of current arrangements in public policies towards democratic governance and education, and to look ahead at the threats facing both in the future.

Threats to guard against

The nightmare that disturbs the sleep of businesspeople, politicians and the bureaucrats of the global system, is one in which the economy ceases to grow and no longer becomes steadily more prosperous. We exaggerate once more, of course, but it is not our aim to develop a full-blown critique of the cultural contradictions of 'turbo-capitalism'. Nor can we describe in detail the efforts of many to articulate other positive options. Geoff Mulgan and Omar Salem,[25] for example, have been working on the theme of well-being (as opposed to happiness) and have placed climate change at the centre of a new kind of politics. They seek to promote local production, arrangements for time-sharing and volunteer banks, and new kinds of carbon-neutral industries at the heart of new circuits of production and consumption. At the centre of their work are ideas about rejuvenating local democracy.

Work such as this has to become part of what Amartya Sen has called 'public reasoning',[26] which he views as a necessary vehicle for social change and economic progress. In our view, the threats we now face arise from the complex interactions in the new world order. Perhaps the most important are listed in Box 2.1.

This is neither a list of priorities nor of predictions, but of topics for debate and action. For educators, it is a debate that should shape our practice with learners. The threats listed prompt questions such as: How can learners be prepared to overcome them collaboratively? How can public reasoning be strengthened? What form do these threats take in particular local settings and how do the responses of people differ?

Box 2.1: Main threats to our collective well-being

1.	Global warming and climate change
2.	Rising and corrosive social, economic and cultural inequalities
3.	The intensification of competition and struggle for scarce resources such as water
4.	Growing differentiation between those who can manage complexity and uncertainty and those who cannot, through no fault of their own
5.	Recurrent crises in capitalism and the failure to regulate financial markets
6.	Corroded civil liberties and the rapid growth of surveillance
7.	Increasingly atrophied images of personal fulfilment, in which mass consumption defines the good life
8.	Spread of extreme ideological politics, often driven by fundamentalist religious conviction that undermines democracy
9.	Rapid emergence of unmanageable outcomes of scientific change, e.g. nuclear accidents and nuclear proliferation
10.	Rise of xenophobic sentiments that dissolve the fragile bonds of human solidarity
11.	The mass media providing us with a deliberately distorted account of the world
12.	The explosive growth of a high-skill but low-wage workforce which breaks the links between education, jobs and the good life

The list in Box 2.1 contains many different kinds of problem. Critical discussion of any one of them will produce new knowledge and promote change, but it depends on an understanding of many different subjects and diverse bodies of information. No one can master all the expertise needed to tackle these challenges. Certainly, it would not be possible to draw from this list a curriculum of 'core knowledge' in which competent citizens should be schooled. It is possible, however, to highlight an important principle that should inform all curricula (in formal education, the workplace and civil society) to help more people to engage in the debate.

The principle is this: knowledge, learning and understanding emerge in a social process in which people discuss, write, and share ideas and expertise. They learn in the course of tackling a real problem together. This is why, of course, both vocational education and active engagement in communities can be such a powerful means of learning. Thoughtful reflection stimulates learning and leads to new ideas, and new ways of thinking and acting that change the reality of people's lives.

The kind of engaged learning we have in mind encourages people to question the circumstances in which they are learning or to make new demands of their educators so that their learning can become more effective.

Some of this is captured in the fashionable idea of 'reflective practice', but not by any means all of it.

We want to go beyond these models and urge the development of **communities of discovery**. We define these as: **groups of people working together democratically to find new ways of responding to the dangers to our collective well-being.**

This definition embraces many different kinds of groups in diverse settings, both public and private. We show in more detail in Chapter 4 the ways in which such communities can be built and how they function. For the moment, it is important to stress this key point: there is a necessary connection between how we judge the threats facing us, that is, what our **diagnosis of our time** is, and the ways in which we approach teaching and learning in all the settings where they take place.

The lack of democracy in our educational institutions

'Why in a democratic society should an individual's first real contact with a formal institution be so profoundly anti-democratic?'[27] Matters have not improved much in the 35 years since that question was asked by Samuel Bowles and Herbert Gintis. Missing from the contemporary debate about education is the need to transform the institutions in which it takes place. Those institutions are designed to reproduce the social, political and economic orders of global capitalism. They do not counter sufficiently strongly the economic and political processes that lie behind the dangerous threats we all face.

For example, the pursuit of economic growth to spread prosperity is highly likely to accelerate uncontrollable global warming. Driving growth forward on the basis of free market globalisation creates the seed-bed conditions in some parts of the world for the growth of religious fundamentalism. That happens because, faced with too much danger and uncertainty, many people become marginalised and defensive, and retreat to the 'safe havens' of their local communities, some of which are based on religious faith.[28]

In our view, current arrangements to promote learning for democracy are inadequate. Young people do not learn in ways that equip them to continue learning, and provisions for lifelong learning remain poorly resourced to meet the learning needs of a vibrant democracy. Despite almost universal secondary education throughout the developed world, there are still high levels of functional illiteracy among adults and young people. In the UK, as a recent study by Sandra McNally and Anna Vignoles[29] has noted, 20 per cent of adults in the UK have inadequate basic skills. The Wolf Report pointed out that '37% of the cohort achieved neither Maths nor English GCSE A*–C at 15…In absolute terms…329,000 at age 15 did not have Maths plus English A*–C; and at age 18, 304,000 still did not'.[30] This means that millions are disadvantaged in their efforts to engage effectively in modern work environments or participate with understanding in politics.

Such problems are not mitigated in the UK by current arrangements for the funding and provision of lifelong learning. The recent national inquiry into the future of lifelong learning by Tom Schuller and David Watson[31] described a system that: skewed expenditure towards the under-25s and seriously underestimated the social importance of the education of adults; reflected wider social inequalities; and prioritised skills-based learning over all kinds of liberal education.

The evidence on which their report is based shows, too, that there have been gains in basic skills in primary schools and in adult education. Using our metaphor from Chapter 1, it is clear that the juggernaut can still be made to go a little faster, but if it is still trundling down the wrong road that is of little help.

Unfortunately, because of the pressures to be policy-relevant and practical, Schuller and Watson's report does not address the need to transform the institutions to which its recommendations are directed. The notion of citizenship that informs its recommendations is also a narrow one. It urges better resources for lifelong learning to enable citizens to engage more effectively with political processes in their localities, but stops short of questioning the democratic validity of the institutions themselves.

The skills of 'civic engagement' that it seeks to promote are certainly desirable. The report's authors wish people to be able to make sense of change, to adapt to it, and to shape its direction. To do this, people must possess 'digital capability', 'health capability', 'financial capability' and 'civic capability'.[32]

We agree with these aims, but these proposals deal with only one side of the problem: the weaknesses in the education of citizens to cope with their world. The other side of it is that the world these citizens must adapt to is divided, dangerous and treats human beings as items of human capital rather than as people with needs, interests and human rights. The educational institutions that prepare people for this world do little to help them imagine other options, and not enough to encourage learners to experience democracy daily in practice so that they can better understand its potentialities.

Schools, colleges and universities are public bodies with a legal identity operating within the law. It is not this that leads to questions about their democratic credentials; it is in the ways they are governed that the deficits appear, for decision-making power is concentrated within governing bodies and senior managers who operate procedures and curricula defined by national bodies. The work they do is not drawn from any radically democratic 'diagnosis of our time'. Quite the contrary: their work is organised to prepare learners for work roles that may well disappear and for a version of democratic citizenship that is very narrowly drawn.

We encourage those who work in formal education and in civil society to assess their organisations against democratic criteria, the most important of which we set out in Box 2.2.

Box 2.2: A democratic audit of our educational institutions

1.	Does the education we offer enable citizens to meet the future threats to our way of life?
2.	Do our educational, social and work organisations enable learners to experience democratic ways of working? Are they engaged in the social and political life of their communities?
3.	Do they encourage the dialogue and public reasoning that leads to new knowledge and social change?
4.	Do our practices respect the human rights of all those we work with?
5.	Do all citizens leave our schools, colleges and universities as lifelong learners who understand how to learn and who can assess their own weaknesses, strengths and enthusiasms as learners?

Ofsted asks colleges of further education 236 questions about leadership, management and the quality of provision, but none are as searching as the five listed above. Yet the latter are important questions, for it is within organisations that respect human rights, promote dialogue and nurture the confidence to contribute to debate that creative new solutions to our problems will emerge.

We present in Box 2.3 (overleaf) a second instrument to help colleagues make an audit of how the main threats affect their locality. We have chosen to emphasise, for each of the issues chosen, the need for knowledge, an understanding of the local context, the means of responding and an estimate of its priority, but colleagues will choose their own themes and the main dimensions to be studied. Box 2.3 is just one way of getting the debate started.

We show in Chapter 4 that there is strong support for this approach. For the moment, our point is this: both effective learning by individuals and new ways of thinking within groups of people emerge only when they are allowed to. New solutions to problems become effective when people are trusted to make their contribution to the common good. In the absence of dialogue, trust and respect in all the settings in which people learn, work and resolve their differences, it is unlikely that shared solutions to collective problems will emerge.

Box 2.3: Local audit of the main threats

MAIN THREATS	Knowledge What do we know about this? What do we need to know? From where and whom can we learn more?	Context How does this manifest itself in our workplace, locality, region and nation?	Process How can we develop innovative and sustainable means of responding to this threat?	Priority What priority should we attach to our work on this threat?
Global warming				
Growing inequalities				
Competition for resources				
Managing complexity				
Undemocratic use of power				
Infringements on liberty and human rights				
Reform of the financial sector				
Political and religious extremism				
Managing scientific risks				
Fear of immigrants				
Unreliability of the mass media				
High-skill but low-wage workforce				

Having credible new solutions to some of the complex problems facing us today is one thing. Turning those ideas into plans for sustainable change that have the support of people is quite another. In a short book written near the end of his life, the British historian Tony Judt reminded us that it was not sufficient just to articulate objections to our way of life:

> As citizens of a free society, we have a duty to look critically at our world. But if we think we know what is wrong, we must **act** upon that knowledge.[33]

In the final chapter of this book we argue that to act on the basis of what we know takes another moral quality: courage. This, too, cannot be taught nor tested as a skill or competence. It is built on self-respect, on the earned respect of others, on the willingness to act in defence of cherished values and on models of courageous behaviour. We need to show young people when to have the courage to **disobey**.

Endnotes

1   Mannheim and Stewart, 1962: 23.

2   Mannheim, 1950.

3   Tawney, 1964: 78.

4   Rees, 2004.

5   Chomsky, 2004.

6   Wolf, 2011: 53.

7   Woodhead, 2009.

8   Tawney, 1964: 105.

9   Wilkinson and Pickett, 2009.

10   Tawney, 1964: 57.

11   Biesta *et al.*, 2011: 14.

12   Nussbaum, 2010; Gutmann and Thompson, 1996; Appiah, 2005, 2010.

13   Sen, 2007; Castells, 1997; Apple, 2000; Grossman, Lee and Kennedy, 2008.

14   Gutmann and Thompson, 1996.

15   Nussbaum, 2010: 18.

16   Wood, 2008: 32; original emphasis.

17   Osler and Starkey, 2006.

18   Scott and Cogan, 2008: 169.

19   Mannheim, 1950: 149.

20   Appiah, 2010.

21   Beveridge, 1942.

22   Mannheim, 1950.

23   Collingwood, 1942.

24   ESRC, 2010.
25   Mulgan and Salem, 2009.
26   Sen, 2007: 53.
27   Bowles and Gintis, 1976: 250.
28   Castells, 1997: 64.
29   McNally and Vignoles, 2010.
30   Wolf, 2011: 84.
31   Schuller and Watson, 2009.
32   Schuller and Watson, 2009: 167–82.
33   Judt, 2010: 237; original emphasis.

Chapter 3

An educational balance sheet

'The most revolutionary thing one can do always is to proclaim loudly what is happening'.

Rosa Luxemburg[1]

Introduction

In this book we present a new way of thinking about education and new ways of acting to bring about radical change, that is, from the very roots upwards. But first we need to produce the evidence that has prompted us to call for a fundamental overhaul rather than detailed revisions of the new policies pouring out of central government. We must, however, warn against their main thrust, for they amount to a determined continuation of the neo-liberal policies that were begun by previous New Labour governments.

The educational policies of the Coalition Government, established in England in 2010, are still evolving. They cover the spectrum of educational provision from pre-school to higher education, and they extend beyond formal education to cover work-based training and apprenticeships. Within this broad remit they cover many detailed topics, such as the curriculum, governance in education, funding, qualifications, new structures (e.g. 'free' schools, university technical colleges, and technology and innovation centres), new models of inspection, standards and assessment. Since May 2010, there has been a cascade of announcements, reviews and directives from the Department for Education and there have been some fierce political battles, especially over the payment of increased fees in higher education, which are to treble to £9,000 per year. Hyperactivity of ministers, with a new initiative every month, which was a marked failing in New Labour administrations, is in danger of undoing the Coalition.

This is not the place to discuss the detail of the policies being developed and enacted. Nor is it our intention to make cheap headline shots that disparage them. Many have done this already, characterising the Government's activities in education after one year as freedoms, cuts and reviews galore. There is some truth in such assertions, but they do not go deep enough. The broad thrust of government policies in all sectors of education is set out in the Coalition Plan for Government.[2] Our task is to highlight two features that are often obscured in the debates about detail or in the orchestrated fury of the headline writers of the press.

The first concerns the underlying rationale of the proposed changes. For behind the policies there is a particular **diagnosis of our time** at work. This incorporates a view of how some members of the Government, together with their powerful ideological backers in right-wing think tanks, in the Tory press and in the bastions of right-wing opinion in Britain, see the future of the country. We wish to make these assumptions explicit.

Second, the policies also contain a view of what they believe is wrong with current educational arrangements and why they wish to change them radically. Tory agendas in education, like those of neo-conservatives elsewhere in the world, particularly in the United States, are much less benign than those of the Liberal Democrats and are concerned with reducing the power of the state in education and opening up the provision of educational services to the competitive discipline of the marketplace and private providers. This is what lies behind their rhetoric of parental choice and diversity of provision in education: the aim is to transfer public funds to the private sector.

They wish to see a return to a 'system' that is differentiated in ways that reflect what they take to be natural and unalterable differences of ability. They wish to see a return to disciplined classrooms, streamed according to ability, and staffed by teachers trained on the job rather than educated in university departments of education. Their view of the curriculum is a reactionary one. They wish to see a return to a traditional curriculum with core academic subjects. The introduction of the ill-named English Baccalaureate, with its emphasis on the core subjects of English, Science, Mathematics, a foreign language and either History or Geography, is the most recent expression of this.

The destructive power of the market – which all neo-conservatives consider to be a creative force that will re-energise what they see as sclerotic state institutions like schools and public hospitals – is to be deployed more extensively in schools and in further and higher education. Their hope is that private providers will drive these services to achieve – at least for the majority of people, if not for those elite groups who can still afford a traditional, high-status, academic education – educational outcomes tailored to the needs of employers and to the Holy Grail of economic growth. We have serious doubts, however, about whether these policies are likely to succeed even on their own narrow terms.

The most effective opposition to them has two elements: first, an affirmation of what is good about existing practice in education in the broad sense in which we defined it in the first chapter; and second, to show that the Government's policies are both a wholly inadequate response to the dangers facing this country and a poor attempt to think imaginatively beyond current possibilities for change. Their plans for an overly academic curriculum, which hark back to the grammar schools of the 1950s, will also do a disservice to those who are considered able enough to study it, precisely because it is backward-looking, and will sideline (and so devalue) subjects like Art, Music, Physical Education, Vocational Education and Technology, which should be integral to everyone's initial education.

There is strong support for some of these policies from right-wing, free-market libertarian groups whose aim is to clip the wings of the state and free up space for private companies to make profits from carrying out public functions. A report from the Adam Smith Institute calls for 'free' schools to become profit-driven.[3] Unlocking the power of profit, the report argues, is the way to drive up standards, particularly for the socially disadvantaged who are particularly ill-served by present-day arrangements. A new grouping called Educators for Reform, part of the right-wing think tank Reform, is promoting the idea that education policies should build on 'the benefits of competition, rigour and elitism'.[4] The Institute of Economic Affairs and Policy Exchange are both pressing a similar agenda: to 'free up' education at all levels to the influence of private providers and reduce state monopolies in education. In their plans, the state retains a residual role as regulator but no longer as 'provider'.

The goal these groups are working towards is that of a free-market society, stressing the values of competition and individual responsibility. The drivers that move such a society to higher levels of economic growth are ambition and self-interest. The belief of those supporting this view, one that flies in the face of the historical and comparative evidence – particularly as exemplified in the world's most unequal societies, such as the United States and the UK, and which is so well documented by Wilkinson and Pickett[5] – is that the benefits of growth 'trickle down' and in this way people are pulled up to higher standards of living. J.K. Galbraith memorably criticised this belief as 'the doctrine that if the horse is fed amply with oats, some will pass through to the road for the sparrows'.[6] In our words, if we are concerned about the welfare of sparrows, we should feed them directly.

What takes our breath away is the failure of the neo-conservatives to learn from the global financial crisis of 2008 when, in Dan Hind's words, 'private self-interest drove the financial system to the point of collapse and state intervention saved it…we struggle under the burden of debts to which we did not consent, the consequences of a crisis we did not cause'.[7] There is no longer any basis in fact for a continuing faith in self-regulating markets as a means of achieving the public good.

System, what system?

The characteristic response of government to any problem (for example, classroom disruption) during the last 60 years has been piecemeal change to existing structures rather than addressing the causes of the problem. As a result, we do not have a coherent or effective 'system', but three uncoordinated and unwieldy sectors, serving primary and secondary schools; post-compulsory education and training; and higher education. This description does not, of course, embrace all the other relevant ways and settings in which people learn, especially in non-formal ways related to their civic participation, and thus policy-makers in government (and too often educators as well) have had a rather limited view of the educational resources of this country.

We want to build on past experiences and current strengths, while addressing the long-standing weaknesses and unjustifiable inequalities within the present 'system'. So we have prepared a balance sheet, where we take stock of English education, while drawing a few appropriate comparisons – and not, we trust, ideologically selected, as government ministers tend to do. Much better, we think, to look to our neighbours in Europe than to follow practice in the USA where, for instance, 'a number of states have now reached a point where they are spending as much public money on prisons as on higher education'.[8] This is not the place for double-entry bookkeeping; instead, we focus only on the outstanding debits and credits, beginning with the latter.

Strengths

When foreign commentators describe what they consider to be the positive aspects of the English model of education, they point to how well that 'system' works for the elite – but this is at the expense of a large, excluded minority and a huge and growing educational gap between the attainments of those at the top and the bottom. They also praise its seemingly inexhaustive capacity for innovation and flexibility, to which we would add resilience. Educationists in this country have been particularly adept at successfully creating new institutions (e.g. the Open University), new structures (e.g. tertiary colleges) and new measures to help the disadvantaged (e.g. Sure Start and Skills for Life).

Schools, colleges and universities have also learned to respond quickly and flexibly to the veritable torrent of government policy, directives and initiatives which has rained down on them with increasing intensity in recent years. New measures, hurriedly introduced by ministers – without any evident knowledge of previous initiatives of a similar kind; or of the current practices of teachers; or of disconfirming evidence from research – have been turned by practitioners into productive opportunities for students. Indeed, the **resilience** of our educational institutions has become one of their greatest strengths: ministers come and go, their initiatives come and go, quangos come and go, the de-schooling movement has come and gone, but our schools, colleges and universities continue to teach students in much the same ways.

This remarkable resilience of our educational institutions needs to be explained. We attribute it to the unselfish commitment of educators to their learners, whom they are determined to protect from all the latest fads, structural changes and centrally imposed initiatives. Where there is success in English education, it can most often be attributed to a strong working relationship between teacher and the taught, to educators who not only know and love their subject, but who also know and care for their learners. For decades, the best of English education has been found in face-to-face teaching in small groups where educators felt a professional responsibility for *all* their students. But such conditions, which are so conducive to educator and students meeting each other as human beings prepared to learn from each other, are becoming rarer, particularly in colleges and universities, because of the sheer pressure of numbers and of demands to cut costs.

Michael Oakeshott – a conservative political philosopher – summed up this point when he argued: 'The only indispensable equipment of "school" is teachers,'[9] and yet successive governments since the 1970s have sought to discipline the 'workforce'. Government after government has squandered the prize asset in education – the goodwill of the teaching profession – by inflating out of all proportion the number of those they regard as incompetent teachers. Yes, there are incompetent teachers, just as there are incompetent doctors, nurses, MPs and Cabinet ministers, and they all need to be dealt with, but their number is small. We wish to speak to the huge majority of committed educators, on whom governments have to rely to enact their policies, but whom they have alienated.

Moreover, from the 1960s to the present, every time educational opportunities have been made available, learners in large numbers have stayed on at school longer, and have gone on to obtain qualifications at FE colleges and universities. Over that period of time, the participation rate in higher education has risen dramatically, from 5 per cent in 1960 to 43 per cent in 2007–08. More recently, the substantially increased investment in education since 1997 has been used in part to provide 2.8 million adults with their first qualifications in literacy and numeracy, helping simultaneously to reduce the stigma of illiteracy and to provide funds for those who have benefited least from the huge expansion in all forms of education. Similarly, in primary and secondary schools, hundreds of thousands more young people than before are now proficient in reading, writing and arithmetic, and have obtained five 'good' GCSEs. All of these achievements are cause for celebration – and the above are just a few of the most outstanding examples of success that we take pleasure in recording.

Another considerable advance took place in 1998 with the publication of the Crick Report on citizenship and the adoption of its main recommendations by government. Since then, citizenship education has been established as an entitlement for all pupils and was defined by the group chaired by Bernard Crick as consisting of three indivisible parts:

- pupils learning socially and morally responsible behaviour
- involving them in the life and concerns of their communities
- learning how to be effective in public life.[10]

The emphasis was to be as much (if not more) on **learning through action** as on discovering how in the past ordinary citizens have been the catalysts for change.

Since the publication of the Crick Report some 13 years ago, there have been some significant advances: citizenship became a compulsory subject in the national curriculum in England; specialist teachers have been appointed in some schools; and 36 organisations throughout the UK have come together to form a coalition:[11]

> to champion citizenship education as the only curriculum subject that teaches young people about their rights and responsibilities as citizens and how young people can participate effectively in our democracy and society.[12]

All this is good news, but the worry now is that this version of citizenship, combining as it does academic knowledge with practical social action, will be dropped by the committee reviewing the curriculum in England: it has not been included, for instance, in the English Baccalaureate (as it is in the International and Welsh Baccalaureates). This young subject, then, has much work still to do, not least because a recent study showed that young people in England had the lowest level of knowledge about the European Union of all the 24 participating European countries.[13]

If the strengths listed above are genuine, how are we to explain the groundswell of dissatisfaction with education which is felt by parents, learners, educators and commentators alike? There are serious weaknesses in the present 'system', which we shall describe next, but they are regularly magnified out of proportion by the open hostility of organised right-wing groups who despise public education, but who nevertheless wish to make profits by taking it over. Our argument is that the successes we have outlined have been bought at too high a cost, not to government or the taxpayer, but at the expense of educators and students. They have had to manage multiple, complex, centre-driven changes to avoid the worst damage they might have inflicted on their institutions. The government-imposed audit of accountability has also turned our schools, colleges and universities into exam factories and businesses, as we shall describe in more detail in Chapter 4.

Weaknesses

Governments both right and left routinely boast that, through their 'drive for excellence', educational standards have risen. Here standards are narrowly defined as increasing test scores; for example, the increased number of students now obtaining five or more 'good' GCSEs at age 16, including English and Maths. The percentage has risen from 45 per cent in 1977 to 67 per cent in 2009. What tends to be ignored in the annual publicity surrounding these improved figures is the 33 per cent who did not gain these qualifications, who are very unlikely ever to get them, and for whom these examinations are seriously inappropriate. As a consequence, each year about 30 per cent of each cohort of young people experience failure and rejection. Some of these students who leave school at 16 with a poor clutch of D, E, F and U grades do not even collect their results, as the dead-end jobs to which they are headed have no need of qualifications.[14]

The recent introduction of the English Baccalaureate into the league tables by which schools are judged has provided the UK Government with ammunition to claim that even the achievements of the past decade are illusory; that educational 'standards' have not really improved so much. Such a way of framing success and failure within education has the effect of both creating even greater, top-down pressure on schools and colleges to raise their game, and of engineering greater social differentiation within educational provision.

Nevertheless, there is a case to consider, especially when the performance of the English educational 'system' is viewed in comparative terms. Among the 28 nations which make up the Organisation for Economic Co-operation and Development (OECD), only Turkey and Mexico have fewer 15 to 19-year-olds in education than England. Even the Department for Education and Skills (as the Department for Education was called in 2004) conceded that this huge dropout rate was 'a scandal'.[15] Since 2004, England's comparative position has improved, but only slightly.

Looking back over the 67 years since the 1944 Education Act, the staggering statistic is that the so-called education 'system' has been failing between 30 per cent and 60 per cent of each generation. Why has this disgraceful outcome been allowed to continue? We suggest the answer is that too many still believe that some people are just 'thick' and should therefore be trained to dig ditches; someone must do the dirty work of society. The previous New Labour Government compounded this historic problem of the long tail of underachievement by introducing a new hierarchy of qualifications, which will increase the division between academic and vocational courses. The new hierarchy consists of:

- the long-established International Baccalaureate and the new Cambridge Pre-U exam for the elite
- A-levels for the middle class

- apprenticeships and employment with training for the skilled working class
- diplomas and now vocational training for the rest – for other people's children.

Indeed, if ministers had set out deliberately to increase social divisions, they would have chosen a qualification like the diplomas because they look as if they were designed for the poor. They are the latest in a long, ignoble history of failed attempts to establish a prestigious vocational route.

This highly expensive and damaging fiasco was the direct result of the Blair Government's refusal to accept the recommendations of the Tomlinson Committee, which argued for a new qualification at 16, one that would have enabled all students to choose their own combination of academic and vocational subjects.[16] Looking back now, that fateful decision appears even more tragic than it did in 2004, because the private schools had agreed to become part of a new national examination that would have replaced GCSEs, A-levels and vocational qualifications with a new single diploma. How many private schools offer diplomas? The answer is none. The figure for the maintained sector is little better. The Wolf Report on vocational education provides the percentage enrolment of the total cohort of 16 to 18-year-olds: it amounted to just 0.6 per cent.[17]

It is, however, the contention of government ministers that we have at least done well by the majority who obtain five or more 'good' GCSEs. If only it were so. The intense pressures, applied by governments to increase test scores, have turned many schools into exam factories rather than learning communities. Young people emerge from 11 years of constant testing better at passing tests but poorer at learning. As a result, too many students now value only what is measured and what leads to qualifications; students have become as narrowly instrumental in their approach as ministers. Too many students are no longer interested in understanding or coming to love the subject they are studying. They are intent on getting as good a qualification as possible so that they can get into a university with a high reputation and increase their chances of an elite job.

The testing regime not only has perverse effects on bright pupils; it also undermines the self-esteem of the less able. Students with a wide range of talents and interests, who in Germany or Sweden would be following prestigious vocational routes, come to view their repeated failure to pass tests as *their* fault; they internalise the message that they are 'thick' and might as well give up trying to learn. It then takes years of slow, dedicated work by staff in FE colleges to convince such young people that they are of value, that they have abilities and can succeed.

At the very bottom of the hierarchy are the million young people aged 16 to 19 who are 'not in education, employment or training' – the so-called 'NEETs'. After 11 years of formal education, they leave school with no qualifications of any kind and want nothing to do with schooling, as they have already suffered too much at its hands.

Governments do not set out deliberately to make matters worse, but that may be the outcome, as they are in thrall to an ideology which is unquestioned, indeed which they treat as unquestionable. We draw a distinction between the **unintended**, perverse consequences of government policy and the highly **foreseeable**, perverse consequences of the actions about which politicians are repeatedly warned but still persist in. The ideology in question is, of course, the market principle and the insistence on competition, regulation and privatisation. We now spend more on inspecting the education sectors than we do on trying to improve them.[18]

When foreign commentators turn to the weaknesses of the English 'system', they point to our repeated bouts of structural change, which do not tackle the fundamental problems of an elite 'system' struggling to modernise itself. One of those fundamental problems remains the deep, unjustifiable inequalities in funding, between primary and secondary schools, between full-time and part-time students, and between further and higher education. We have space to deal only with the last of these inequalities. Alison Wolf has provided detailed evidence of the dramatic contrast between government expenditure on student support in FE and HE in England in 2008–09. In FE, support for learners aged 19 and over amounted to £167 million; in HE the figure was £3,981 million.[19]

Throughout this book we have referred to the English 'system', always in inverted commas, because as we argued earlier, we do not have an education **system**, but three badly coordinated **sectors** which reflect sharp social distinctions in English society, and which are replicated within Whitehall and university departments of education. The Panel on Fair Access to the Professions reported, for instance, that 'there are more students of black Caribbean origin at London Metropolitan University than at all the Russell Group universities combined'.[20]

The deeply elitist culture of these institutions has remained virtually intact despite strenuous attempts by almost a decade and a half of New Labour administrations to get them to open their doors to a broader section of the population. Moreover, the same Panel reviewed the evidence on social mobility and came to the conclusion that it had stalled in recent years and that 'social mobility in the UK is generally lower than in many other countries'.[21] One statistic conveys this message all too powerfully: after 140 years of a so-called national 'system' of education, there are still no recognised routes from apprenticeships to higher education. Since 1997 more than two million people have started an apprenticeship, but only 2,000 (or 0.2 per cent) of them made it into higher education, which just goes to show that in the UK most people continue to receive an education suited to their class rather than to their abilities.[22]

Alison Wolf has also recorded the bizarre fact that, for years, taxpayers have been subsidising employers by paying for their firm-specific training. In 2007–08, for example, out of a total of £714 million spent on Train to Gain, £910,000 was given to McDonalds and £465,105 to BP Oil UK Limited. These huge investments in training might be worthwhile, if, in accordance with the Government's central belief, they had led to improved levels of productivity: unfortunately, 'there has been no increase in the trend growth of British productivity since 1997'.[23] No wonder Wolf concluded her assessment of the evidence as follows:

> The current system is opaque, wasteful, unjust, fails to achieve its own narrow economic objectives and is effectively unreformable.[24]

Summing up

On the plus side, we see three innovative, responsive and resilient sectors, where educators work hard to ensure that learners are protected from the hyperactivity of ministers and the hyper-accountability they have imposed. Over the last 40 years, all three sectors have expanded, and many more young people and adults stay in education for longer and achieve qualifications, some for the first time, as adults. These are significant strengths out of which a new and more democratic, just and coherent 'system' needs to grow.

But first we need to address the debit side of the balance sheet. We have described a dysfunctional, disorganised and demoralised public service which is being held together by the goodwill of its educators. Politicians from all the main parties claim that 'more of the same' or, more accurately, 'more with less' will make us 'world class' in education.

Politicians and senior civil servants want to continue with a testing regime that fails a sizeable minority of each generation of young people. The unstated assumption behind their policies is that the poor can remain in long-term unemployment, in sub-standard housing on 'sink estates', with all the attendant health and psychological problems; and yet miraculously their children are expected to perform as well at school as the children of the middle classes with their private tutors, foreign holidays, books, computers and intimate knowledge of how the educational sectors work. We know from longitudinal studies of a nationally representative sample that by the age of 3, children from disadvantaged homes are educationally up to a year behind children from privileged backgrounds.[25]

Those who pass the tests and gain qualifications are not independent, critical thinkers who know how to take responsibility for their own learning, because they have not had the opportunity to play such a role. What British industry and society need are innovative, reflective learners who can think for themselves; what the present model produces, for those who obtain access to further and higher education, is young people who can reproduce what others have said or thought.

This is at a time when, as Kimberley Seltzer and Tom Bentley's[26] work on creativity showed, we know that the long-term survival of the UK economy demands a curriculum that nurtures creativity. The introduction of the market principle into education has created 'a new moral environment' where schools, colleges and universities are inducted into 'a culture of self interest [and] survivalism', which shifts concern away from the public good to the protection of the institution and its members.[27] The long-term survival of a democratic political order capable of dealing with the threats that all modern societies now face, demands citizens who have a critical understanding of their institutions and both a willingness and an ability to imagine different ways to run the country and its policies. As we know, through no fault of theirs, schools fail on both counts.

Since the financial crash of 2008, we realise that economic recovery needs more than well-educated, innovative employees. We know that, especially in the financial sectors, there is a great need for public accountability, democratic management and a radically reframed understanding of the purposes of economic activity **and of education.**

What is needed is a new idea of what a different 'system' could be, were it built on clear, democratic principles and practices with open possibilities for creative collaboration among all educators. We offer an outline of an alternative in the next chapter. Sclerosis, however, sets in when the powerful are allowed to claim they know what is needed and inflict their will on the rest of us.

Endnotes

1   Quoted in Hind, 2008: 147.
2   HM Government, 2010.
3   Croft, 2011.
4   See http://www.reform.co.uk
5   Wilkinson and Pickett, 2009.
6   Galbraith, 1992: 27.
7   Hind, 2010: 3.
8   Wilkinson and Pickett, 2009: 27.
9   Oakeshott, 2001: 71.
10   QCA, 1998.
11   See http://www.democraticlife.org.uk
12   Democratic Life, 2011: 3.
13   IEA, 2010.

14 Coffield, Borrill and Marshall, 1986.

15 DfES, 2004: 71.

16 Tomlinson, 2004.

17 Wolf, 2011: 56.

18 The inspection service, Ofsted, which covers primary, secondary, post-compulsory and children's services, will cost £176 million in 2011–12. The total budget of the Learning and Skills Improvement Service for the post-compulsory sector is £56 million for the same year.

19 Wolf, 2009: 129. Information about per capita expenditure is not available.

20 Panel on Fair Access to the Professions, 2009: 89. The Russell Group consists of 20 universities, including Bristol, Cambridge, Cardiff, Glasgow, Manchester, Oxford, Imperial College London and three colleges of the University of London.

21 Panel on Fair Access to the Professions, 2009: 36.

22 DBIS, 2009: 10.

23 Wolf, 2009: 51.

24 Wolf, 2009: 144.

25 Centre for Longitudinal Studies, 2007.

26 Seltzer and Bentley, 1999.

27 Ball, 2008: 45.

Chapter 4

From exam factories to communities of discovery

'The good teacher imparts a satisfying explanation, the great teacher …unsettles, bequeaths disquiet, invites argument'.

Richard Sennett[1]

The need for a new approach

When 16-year-olds in Germany decide to start an apprenticeship in order to become an electrician, a carpenter or a nursery nurse, they sign a contract with an employer and a vocational college which sets out the training and work experience they will receive and the commitment expected in terms of hours. In addition, the first sentence of the contract reads: 'The main purpose of this apprenticeship is to make you an active citizen of a democracy'. Meanwhile, in the UK the height of our ambition is to offer apprentices 'employability skills' so that they keep themselves in a state of permanent readiness via constant retraining for work, should they find any.

Our schools, colleges and universities have been turned into **exam factories**, where teaching to the test and gaining qualifications and learning techniques to pass exams are now what matters, rather than understanding, or being interested in, or loving, the subjects being studied. Stress levels are running high among educators and students, and all this pain is being endured in the cause of improving the international competitiveness of British business.

One voice, however, is not heard in the public debates on education: the voice of educators, who are the only people who can enact the reforms but whose involvement in their formation has been reduced to the empty ritual of a consultation exercise. It would be considered very radical to suggest that in England teachers' representatives (that is, the unions) should be equal parties in policy formation, but that is standard procedure in countries like Germany,

Sweden and Finland. As we have argued in earlier chapters, our educational institutions have remained deeply undemocratic, but nothing in the 'system' is as undemocratic as the policy process itself, which in England remains the exclusive preserve of politicians and their chosen advisers.

This is not the place to provide a detailed assessment of the evidence that points to the damage which is being done by the overly rigorous testing regime in England; those who wish to consult that evidence are directed to Frank Coffield's 2010 paper.[2] Here we will simply indicate some of its baleful effects at three levels: the 'system'; schools, colleges and universities; and staff and students.

A central feature of the exams industry that has grown up in the UK, and which deserves much closer public scrutiny, is the role of the 144 awarding bodies, which offer qualifications at GCSE, A-level and in all vocational areas. In all, there are now over 9,700 different accredited qualifications.[3] The exam fees that schools and colleges pay to the awarding bodies have turned assessment into a billion pound industry, with organisations like Edexcel earning huge profits for Pearson plc from the explosive expansion of vocational qualifications from 66,000 in 2003 to 500,000 in 2010. The awarding bodies, however, are not only a financial cost on schools and colleges, they are also a heavy administrative burden because of their different demands and procedures. It does not have to be like this: in Germany, qualifications are developed, run and awarded by a government body, which brings together all the social partners – experienced practitioners, educationists and trade unionists as well as employers and civil servants.

Educational policy in England becomes ever more extreme: no other country in the world subjects its pupils to such an extensive battery of national tests. Government policy on testing, as enacted by both Conservative, New Labour and now Coalition administrations, has resulted in teaching to the test; a narrowing of the curriculum; teachers being forced, often against their wishes and values, to adopt methods of transmitting information to pupils in order to 'cover' overfull curricula; and a serious neglect of those pupils who are unlikely to meet the official target of five 'good' GCSEs.

The Coalition Government is also tightening the straitjacket by introducing more stringent criteria by which schools are to be judged. For example, the minimum percentage of passes at GCSE that the Government considers acceptable is being increased from 30 per cent to 35 per cent in 2010–11, to 40 per cent in 2011–12, and to over 50 per cent by 2015. This will enlarge the number of 'failing' schools which can then be privatised. The English Baccalaureate requires schools to offer all pupils a particular set of subjects by which they will be assessed, and thus the value of subjects not included in the English Baccalaureate is diminished; and the perfectly sensible practice of allowing students to resit exams until they reach the required standard is to be abandoned.

We could learn from the experience of Diane Ravitch, who was Assistant Secretary of Education in the administration of President George H.W. Bush in the 1990s. She subsequently became disillusioned with the strategies of national testing and accountability, which 'once seemed so promising [but which] turned into a nightmare for American schools, producing graduates who were drilled regularly on the basic skills but were often ignorant about almost everything else'.[4] High-stakes testing and punitive regimes of accountability have, in her considered view, 'transformed' education in American public schools, but very much for the worse.

Back in the UK, at an institutional level, a head of a highly successful comprehensive school openly admitted: 'We are an exam factory. I have no issue with that'.[5] Well, we do. We understand that heads, threatened by government with school closure if their exam results are poor, have responded to this intense pressure by stressing test scores above all other considerations. But let us not pretend that these pupils are receiving an education. Heads pass the pressure down the system to their staff by demanding before an Ofsted inspection that only the highest grades across the board will do. The main driving force for change in England has become fear: fear of poor exam results, fear of poor inspection grades, fear of sliding down the national league tables, and fear of public humiliation and closure. Fear is inimical to learning.

Stephen Ball has summarised the effects of hyper-accountability on tutors in schools, colleges, community centres and universities: increased emotional pressures and stress; intensification of workloads; a decline in sociability among staff; an increase in the production of data for management; greater surveillance of their teaching and its outcomes; and:

> a developing gap, in values, purpose and perspective, between senior staff, with a primary concern with balancing the budget, recruitment, public relations and impression management, and teaching staff, with a primary concern with curriculum coverage, classroom control, students' needs and record keeping.[6]

The impact on students has been to make them mark-hungry, obsessed with exams, and physically and emotionally stressed. They have become expert passers of tests, who have little time for, or interest in, subjects or topics that are not examined, and who are adept at regurgitating 'unwanted answers to unasked questions'.[7] Too many have become highly dependent learners who expect to be spoon-fed. (At one college we were told staff no longer spoon-feed their students to help them succeed: 'Here we breast-feed them'.) Government policy again heaps on the pressure, because in 2011–12 over 583,000 applicants are chasing 400,000 places on degree courses. Those who will have to reapply next year will have to repay tuition fees of £9,000 a year rather than £3,375 at present – a total of £27,000 over three years. Moreover, students know that getting an A at A-level is no longer good enough to secure a place at an elite university – they must obtain an A*. Is it any wonder that increasing numbers are prescribed medication to help with the stress?[8] When will parents, educators and students reach the point when these pressures are widely considered to be intolerable?

That point, we reckon, will come sooner rather than later and, when it does, we will need a well-thought-out alternative, which is sound in both theory and practice. We want to start a public debate on what that alternative should be, by describing now in more detail what we mean by communities of discovery, how they can be built, what lessons we can learn from successful education at the periphery of the 'system', and the role of the new technologies in building democracy.

Main features of communities of discovery

We need a metaphor and a model of change that are more genuinely democratic. We propose that over time our educational institutions work towards becoming communities of discovery, some of the main characteristics of which we list in Box 4.1, and then outline below that.

Box 4.1: Main features of communities of discovery

1.	Educators and learners are not 'providers' and 'consumers' but partners in learning.
2.	All educators are learners and all learners are educators.
3.	Learning is the central organising principle of the 'system', sector and institution.
4.	Principled dissent is positively encouraged.
5.	Educators and students have the intellectual and physical space in which to grow.
6.	Everyone can improve the quality of their work.
7.	Learning will be mainly collaborative, based on dialogue.
8.	The learning environment is expansive rather than restrictive.
9.	Educational institutions should be run on educational principles, not management nostrums.
10.	Even large, complex institutions can become communities of discovery.
11.	Educational institutions become the thriving hubs of local communities.
12.	We all have three democratic rights in education – to individual enhancement, to be included and to participate.
13.	Power is more widely, equally and openly shared among members.

1. Educators and learners treat each other not as 'providers' and 'consumers' but as human beings, who come together to pursue knowledge and understanding as trusted and mutually respecting partners.

2. All educators are learners and all learners are educators.

3. Learning becomes the central organising principle of the 'system', the sector and the institution. The relationship between, on the one hand, government and government agencies and, on the other, institutional leaders is not that of a parent dealing petulantly with wayward children (as it has been in recent years), but one of full and equal partners. The post-compulsory sector prides itself in always having been responsive to government initiatives. We would like to suggest that it has become *too* responsive. Successful partnerships require all parties to be strong enough to balance competing interests among the members. So we would like to see the principals and governors of FE colleges, as a body, standing up to government on a matter of educational principle. In turn, we expect all senior managers to treat their colleagues in the same way as they expect those colleagues to treat learners.

4. Principled dissent by staff and students is not only tolerated, it is positively encouraged. Learners (and leaders) grow by being challenged, and institutions become mature when members at all levels are able to tell truth to power. Ministers, institutional leaders and educators need to learn not just to tolerate constructive criticism, but to use it to improve their performance. Our new curriculum should nurture in all young people a creative discontent with current social, economic, political and environmental conditions.

5. Educators and students have the intellectual and physical space in which to experiment with new ideas and techniques, and to make mistakes in the constant search for improvement. They view their work as a 'shared experiment, [as a] collective exercise in trial and error'.[9] Learning to work well in teams shows them how to become active, cooperative citizens in civil society.

6. All members of the community of discovery are considered to have the ability to do good work, and they improve the quality of their work because they want to become better at learning; in other words, they improve for the sake of improving, not to pass a test or receive a bonus. Educators who want to be more than just employees take pride in their teaching, in their research (where appropriate), in the achievements of all their students and in what they learn from them.

7. We need more **collaborative** learning, based on dialogue, to release the social and creative resources of our educators, learners, institutions and communities. All citizens need to be given the vocabulary and the abilities to engage in public debates about the issues that concern them. In the words of Robin Alexander: 'Democracies need citizens who can argue, reason, challenge, question, present cases and evaluate them. Democracies decline when citizens listen rather than talk, and when they comply rather than debate.'[10] He makes a persuasive case for giving dialogue the central role in classes from primary schools to adult education, and he bases his case on the following principles: dialogue is **collective** (educators and students learn together); **reciprocal** (they listen to each other); **supportive** (they help each other to understand); **cumulative** (they build on each others' ideas); and **purposeful** (dialogue is not pleasant chit-chat, but moves towards specific educational goals). Dialogue also introduces more equal power relations because if you ask challenging questions, you must be prepared to answer them, especially when you do not yet know the answer.

8. Lorna Unwin and Alison Fuller make the interesting point that educational institutions tend not to see themselves as workplaces, and their research has shown that the quality of learning in workplaces is likely to lie along a continuum from expansive to restrictive. Educational institutions as well as companies need to become more dynamic sites for learning, where one of the key roles of managers is to support the learning of their employees, rather than meeting targets. **Expansive learning** develops the abilities of *all* employees, whose experience and expertise are built on; mentoring and coaching are widely used; high levels of discretion and trust are accorded to all workers; and informal learning is valued as a means of sharing and creating new knowledge. In contrast, **restrictive workplaces** make few connections between on and off-the-job learning; time spent on reflection is seen as unproductive; and learning centres are impersonal, and dominated by computers. In sum, the learning needs of individuals and organisations are brought into positive alignment in expansive settings so that 'they form a powerful force for organisational change'.[11] One of New Labour's successful initiatives was the training of 23,000 union learning representatives (ULRs), who in 2008–09 helped over 220,000 workers into learning.[12] In short, ULRs have been able to reach parts of the workforce that no one has been able to reach before.

9. Our educational institutions should be run on educational principles rather than on the highly questionable nostrums of management, such as branding, total quality control and performance management. Teaching is seen as a noble and essential profession, so neither government nor

government agencies tell teachers how to teach. In 1991, Kenneth Clarke, as Secretary of State for Education, argued that 'questions about how to teach are not for Government to determine'.[13] Since then, the national literacy and numeracy strategies in primary schools, which lay down what and how teachers should teach, have become, to all intents and purposes, mandatory.

10. Large, complex and unwieldy institutions like colleges of FE or universities, which can have upwards of 50 separate departments or units, face particular problems in transforming themselves into communities of discovery. Such mega-institutions can, however, exemplify the spirit of these proposals in the way they exercise power, through creating a trusting and collaborative climate; in the way *all* members of staff – from cleaner to chancellor – are treated with respect, trained and developed; and in the way all have the opportunity to participate in making the decisions that most affect them.

11. It remains the case, however, that most formal learning does not take place in institutions, but in classrooms and workplaces 'as a result of the daily, minute-to-minute interactions that take place between teachers and students and the subjects they study'.[14] It follows that the attempt to transform the quality of learning needs to concern itself not only with the systems within which classrooms are embedded, but also with changing the practice of educators in thousands of classrooms up and down the country. Here we must confront the problems of scale, complexity and repeated failure. A good start will be made if educators are released from the private world of the classroom to create partnerships with those teaching the same subjects in neighbouring schools or colleges;[15] and with local businesses, universities and community leaders. So the school is opened up to educative influences from local museums, fire and police stations, supermarkets and small traders, banks and factories, theatres and restaurants. The educational institution becomes in effect the joyful, thriving hub of the local community, integrated with the worlds of work, culture and leisure.

12. At the heart of these communities of discovery, we will need new democratic methods of teaching and learning that can grow gradually from those successes within the current model, such as the practices of youth workers and union learning reps. There are, however, some minimum conditions for building our new communities of discovery, as Basil Bernstein argued when he described three basic rights that everyone should enjoy in education. His framework, presented in Box 4.2, also provides us with a set of principles to evaluate democracy in our schools, colleges and universities.

Box 4.2: Democratic rights in education

RIGHTS	CONDITIONS	LEVELS
Enhancement	Confidence	Individual
Inclusion	Community	Social
Participation	Civic practice	Political

Source: Adapted from Bernstein, 1996: 7.

Our first right is the right to **individual enhancement**, that is the right 'to be *more* personally, *more* intellectually, *more* socially, *more* materially [enhanced]; it is the right to the means of critical understanding and to new possibilities'.[16] This right operates at an individual level and provides the confidence with which to act.

Our second right is 'to **be included** socially, intellectually, culturally and personally [which] may also require the right to be separate, to be autonomous'.[17] This right operates at the social level and creates the condition for a vibrant community.

Our third right is to **participate**; not just in discussions, but in those practices which construct, maintain or transform the social and political order. This right operates at the political level and provides the condition for everyone to be involved in the collective task of shaping the future of their society.

It is now an empirical question to examine 'whether *all* students receive and enjoy such rights or whether there is an unequal distribution of those rights'.[18] We know, however, from previous chapters that there are seriously unequal distributions of knowledge, resources and access, which affect the rights of particular groups of learners to the three rights of enhancement, inclusion and participation. Some students, mainly those from already advantaged backgrounds, are more valued and financially supported than others, as is evident in the huge disparities in per pupil funding in primary as opposed to secondary schools, and in FE colleges as opposed to universities, not to mention in the leading private schools. Nor is it enough for learners to take part in the running of institutions as they now are; they must experience the processes of improving them and be given a working understanding of the mechanisms of democratic change because the task of renewal will be different for each generation.

13. The issue that lies behind all the discussion so far is power. In communities of discovery, power is widely and more equally shared among members, whose main task is the formation of active citizens in a democracy. Power, like poverty, is best seen as a relationship between people, and the

question will be asked whether there can ever be full equality between teacher and the taught. The answer which the English philosopher Anthony O'Hear gives is that:

> Education cannot be democratic…because educating involves imparting to a pupil something which he [sic] has yet to acquire… Education, then, is irretrievably authoritarian and paternalist [sic]… Education cannot be egalitarian. It has to claim authority, and to recognise, promote and defer to elites.[19]

This is the voice of the self-appointed, gender-blind master who has never doubted that he himself is one of the elite and who sees himself as so superior in intellect and standing to his students that he demands deference from them. In communities of discovery, students are no longer the passive recipients of information imparted by a master or mistress but learning partners. On this point, we take our stance from A.H. Halsey:

> If you are a teacher and I come to learn, then your knowledge must have authority over my ignorance; but again, the school you run is successful precisely in so far as it brings me to competent citizenship in the trade, profession or subject you teach me; and from that moment I can claim the right to democratic relations with you.[20]

Our mental image of the relationship between tutor and student is that of a **tandem bike**. For the bike to move as fast as it can, both cyclists need to coordinate their efforts, especially at the start, to ensure they are 'in sync' with one another. The aim of the tutor, which is made clear to the student right from their first meeting, is that as soon as possible the student should become the lead cyclist at the front.

Building communities of discovery

The idea of a community of discovery is both a theoretical and an intensely practical one. We have tried to imagine the ways in which groups of people can come together to discover new ways of working that will enrich their understanding and practice of democracy. An important element in building such a community is the need for participants to share openly their ideas about how they think it should work; and to make explicit at the outset the basis on which they are approaching the problems they are thinking about.

Our interest is in democratic education, and the history of science provides many clues about how to develop it. It is a long, inspiring and complex story from which we take four ideas that enrich the idea of a community of discovery in a practical way.

First, scientific discovery often occurs when it is needed, when old approaches to a problem no longer explain the phenomena being studied.[21] We take from this that a necessary element of the work of a community of discovery is for its members to be well informed in a critical way about their field of expertise. They, like scientists, have to be constantly open to the idea that their current understanding of their practice is in some ways likely to be inadequate and therefore needs to be improved.

Second, scientific knowledge grows when well-informed people come together to share their ideas. In other words, educators have much to learn from one another; collaborative work across academic and organisational boundaries is something to be encouraged; and the good work of individual, reflective practice can feed into a stream of collective discovery. This will not happen without people coming together in an organised way to consolidate, research and disseminate what they have come to know.

Third, there is little point in managing education solely on the basis of what we think we currently know. Following the fashionable doctrine of 'evidence-based practice' is a recipe for repeating all our past mistakes. To return to our earlier analogy, we have a lot of evidence-based practice about how to improve the mechanical performance of a juggernaut on our congested roads. Such evidence provides no answer as to how we might build a transport system better suited to our needs. If we start out with a limited idea of what citizenship means, then the curricula we create to help people understand it will reflect its limitations. It will not be fit for the purpose of making sense of the modern world in the fresh ways that are clearly needed.

Fourth, the essential character of scientific knowledge, as opposed to religious or political belief, is that it is, in principle, capable of being disproved. In this sense, scientific knowledge is provisional and scientists who are true to the spirit of their discipline are willing to change even their most cherished views in the light of new evidence.

From this we draw a political conclusion. New ideas do not grow like flowers according to some natural plan; they emerge through processes of struggle. The long struggle – Raymond Williams called it 'the long revolution'[22] – for free, state-provided education is a case in point. At each stage in the process, the pioneers of reform had to overcome the resistances of tradition, of elite power determined to keep education exclusive, or of economic arguments that it could not be afforded, or the psychological arguments that few had the ability to benefit. As Michael Fielding and Peter Moss[23] have recently shown, the history of modern education is punctuated with the achievements of researchers, educators and innovators who discovered how to overcome, remove or work around the barriers that prevented people from gaining an education.

Lessons from the periphery

We have been impressed over many years by the work we have seen being done with young people who are on the periphery of formal education, often through being excluded or who are being helped back into education through the youth justice system. We know, too, of the pioneering education work that goes on *in extremis* in prisons or among people driven to the edges of society through unemployment, depression and other forms of mental illness.

The fact that some of the best work with disengaged young people goes on outside schools in youth and community agencies is telling. The fact also that the well-researched evaluations of such work rarely feed back into the practice of schools and colleges is also telling. There is a vast body of work in the UK, arising from decades of publicly funded local initiatives to re-engage disaffected young people with learning, to promote access to education among socially disadvantaged communities and to deal innovatively with young offenders. The organisations involved – some public, like youth justice teams or the Connexions service; some charitable, like the Prince's Trust or the Rathbone Foundation – have exemplified in their work some of the main features of communities of discovery.

The content and methods of teaching which emerge from this work stress the importance of treating young people with respect; of engaging them in discussions about what they want to learn and how they wish to do so; of not inferring a young person's capacity from their current performance. The general theme for those working with marginalised young people is that the best results come from projects that people join of their own free will and where the rules governing how people learn and work together are negotiated by agreement. Such work demands a flexible curriculum and non-specific targets of achievement. It is mutual trust and open-ended searching for mutual understanding and joint development that govern what people do together, not externally imposed targets of performance.

Formal education cannot simply take some of the best ideas from these peripheral initiatives. This is prevented by: the structure and organisation of schools; state management of resources; targets; and the power of well-organised parents to demand what they believe is a traditional, high-quality academic education. Educators in different organisations can, if they choose to do so, learn from these initiatives, liaise with their coordinators, collaborate with them and test out new ways to meet the needs of a more diverse student community.

Missing from many of these projects is any way of recording or consolidating what has been learned. They experience high staff turnover, short-term funding and poor coordination. What they have come to know does not get passed on through well-managed programmes of personal and professional development. With appropriate interventions at a higher level, say by a democratic local authority, arrangements could be put in place to enable such consolidation to take place.

Information, knowledge and democracy

Open, unconstrained communication is one of the key ingredients of a community of discovery. The possibilities that have been opened up by the internet are beyond anything that could have been imagined two decades ago, and new uses for digital democracy are being discovered on a daily basis.

New technologies enable the rapid collation and transmission of information to take place and so can enrich the resources of every classroom or training room. The public libraries of today have a global reference section. The new technologies make possible new, open curricula that in principle can be made available all over the world. Now learners are no longer just receivers of information, but can become active players in its production and dissemination. In Victoria Carrington's words, we should be 'celebrating the ability, or more importantly the right [of students] to produce, disseminate and comment on information'.[24]

Open universities across the world enable students to study for qualifications without leaving their own countries. The Massachusetts Institute of Technology is currently claiming that course materials for over 2,000 of its courses are now available on the web.[25] The Open Knowledge Foundation, set up in 2004 in Cambridge UK, is a not-for-profit organisation that seeks to bring people together to share data of all kinds (scientific, literary, historical) to make it more accessible. Wikipedia is an example of the kind of development the Foundation has in mind to promote. There are other groups and organisations, such as the Open Science Summit, based at the University of California, Berkeley, which was formed last year to bring together professionals and amateurs to undertake research, free from the constraints imposed by the conventional, corporate funders of science.

About the work of such groupings we can only be sure of this: it will grow. It will cover all domains of knowledge and that will challenge the currently privileged positions of schools, colleges, universities and professional bodies and governments as the guardians and filters of public knowledge. Because young people, more than adults, tend to keep up with the latest advances in technology, the power relationship between them is shifting slowly but surely in favour of younger learners. Improvements in teaching and learning, however, will not come from technology but from educators and students, working together.

People are learning to use the world wide web and other digital technologies to transform politics too. Political campaigns can quickly build within and across national boundaries. The Arab Spring of 2011 is a startling and inspiring example of this. Hundreds of thousands of protesters were able to organise, mobilise and shake dictatorial regimes to the core. People who had never previously engaged in political activity were able to do so. Such developments will increase and it will no longer be possible for governments to control the information that people have access to. IT-savvy young people in particular are becoming politically engaged as never before.

The new technologies do, of course, have their dark side. Wikipedia, for example, is not free of political distortion. The blogosphere has no agreed rules of democratic debate. The web overflows with sites promoting crazy, malevolent causes as well as others that are professionally developed, promoting well-focused, well-informed but nevertheless ideologically driven causes across all domains of public policy and international affairs. Powerful lobby groups can shape media messages in ways that directly influence public opinion, and new social networks such as Facebook can be – and are – used to bully vulnerable people and to spread pornography.

Given this, it is vital that a strong case is made for the development of digital literacy that is rooted in a critical understanding of how different claims to truth can be judged. We cannot all be professional philosophers, but we all now need an education that not only equips us to use modern digital communications skilfully, but also enables us to discriminate between information and knowledge, between reasoned argument, based on evidence, and promotional material within the 'unfiltered cacophony of opinions' on the internet.[26] We all need the ability to challenge the pretentious promises of politicians, the patronising hype of advertisers and the overblown claims of experts, including, at times, professors of education. We need, in short, the ability to detect bullshit and the moral courage to expose it.

To enable us to do that, we urgently need a reform of the mass media on which we depend for our information because they do not give us a reliable account of the world:

> *The coverage that preceded the invasion of Iraq in 2003 and the breakdown of the financial system in 2007–08 demonstrated the systemic unreliability of the media.[27]*

It is not appropriate to expand here on Dan Hind's appealing plan for reforming the commissioning and dissemination of public knowledge, except to say that giving the public the power to commission journalists and scientists to investigate matters chosen by the general population seems a very close approximation to our notion of a community of discovery.

Endnotes

1   Sennett, 2008: 6.

2   Coffield, 2010.

3   Lee, 2010.

4   Ravitch, 2010: 2.

5   Curtis, 2009.

6   Ball, 2008: 52.

7   Popper, 1976: 40.

8   Shepherd, 2011a: 10.

9   Sennett, 2008: 288.

10   Alexander, 2006: 37.

11   Unwin and Fuller, 2003: 23.

12   DBIS, 2009: 6.

13   Quoted in Alexander, 2010: 291.

14   Thompson and Wiliam, 2007: 1.

15   See Fielding *et al*, 2005, on the development of joint practice.

16   Bernstein, 1996: 6; original emphasis.

17   Bernstein, 1996: 6.

18   Bernstein, 1996: 6.

19   O'Hear, 1991: 5 and 47.

20   Halsey, 1986: 186.

21   The rationale for this observation comes from Kuhn, 1962.

22   Williams, 1965.

23   Fielding and Moss, 2011.

24   Carrington, 2008: 162.

25   See Johnson, 2011.

26   David Horsey, quoted by Goodlad, 2008: 20.

27   Hind, 2010: 107.

Chapter 5

Can we do it?

'The key is to map out ways in which the new society can begin to grow within and alongside the institutions it may gradually marginalise and replace'.

Richard Wilkinson and Kate Pickett[1]

Learners as citizens

The policy-maker asks the reasonable question: 'What works?' and expects practical answers that can be implemented quickly and successfully. We prefer the more realistic approach implied in 'Can we do it?', but a better question still is: 'In what democratic ways can educators and learners move from exam and skills factories towards a more just and sustainable education for all?' This question invites imaginative, new answers not constrained either by current practices in formal education, which are obsessed with testing, qualifications and competitiveness, or those practices in the world of work focused on skills and competencies. It invites us to think about what education might be, rather than what it has become.

The changes that are needed begin with an acknowledgement that learners – at all levels and across all age groups – are citizens with human rights. From this, it follows that opportunities for learning at all stages of life are a necessary feature of an open, democratic society to which citizens have an entitlement, and therefore should be free. The costs of providing such opportunities will be paid back in abundance by socially responsible citizens engaged in a lifetime of creative work and civic engagement.

Successful learning requires human relations between educators and learners that are freely chosen, based on trust and mutual respect, in which learners feel safe, supported and then challenged, so that they become better at learning. So learning about citizenship is not simply a matter of pursuing a course of study. It is an experience and a practice that changes our identities; we become citizens when we are treated and valued as citizens.

Much contemporary practice in schools, universities, communities and workplaces is very far removed from this ideal. Scottish specialists in the practice of community education Jim Crowther and Ian Martin put it this way: 'There has been a lot of talk about teaching citizenship but much less about learning democracy. This seems to be putting the cart before the horse'.[2]

It is now over ten years since the publication of the Crick Report[3] on citizenship and, despite many schools carrying out the spirit and the letter of the Crick recommendations, we would still contend that too few citizens would conclude that they either attended a school run on democratic principles or that they are living in a democracy where their views are considered, never mind acted upon. While we were writing this book, we came across examples of a council of teachers and pupils in a comprehensive school that did not allow pupils to discuss the wearing of school uniform in case they came to a conclusion different from the one the senior staff wanted; and of a headteacher, in the midst of the most severe winter for 30 years, excluding pupils for wearing boots rather than regulation black shoes. The head explained on television that if pupils were allowed to break one rule, then chaos would ensue.

The major complaint from pupils, even those aged 16 to 18, continues to be that they are not active participants in class, but passive recipients of information.[4] We need to break away from the passionless transmission of inert information, by choosing instead to study both the crucial problems faced by our culture and our procedures for thinking and acting on them. For instance, learners of all ages may wish to know how the richest 1 per cent of people in the UK earn more than 12 per cent of gross national income, which enables them to send their children to private schools, where often the cost per child for fees alone is more than the national average wage of £26,000. We are not, as Tory politicians in the UK like to claim, 'all in this together'. The costs of austerity and inequality are borne disproportionately by the least well off, while the rich remain largely unaffected.

Citizens also need to know how the three main political parties are going to tackle the deep-seated and escalating inequalities that have been exposed yet again by the National Equality Panel (2010). As the chair of that Panel argued: 'Wealth makes a huge difference to people's ability to afford houses in the catchment areas of the best schools, private tutors or private education, and to help finance the master's degrees essential for some jobs, or to help children get on the housing ladder'.[5] Topics such as these would enliven the curriculum, as would enquiries into unemployment, because for many adults having a well-paid job worthy of a human being would be a more potent symbol of citizenship than voting every four years. The million young people under 25 who are currently unemployed and who have little prospect of decent jobs with training also wish to know what stake they have in this society.

Challenges

Finally, we want to tie together the main strands of our argument by assessing both the **challenges** that all educators will face in attempting to realise our recommendations, and the **opportunities** that will facilitate their acceptance and enactment. Box 5.1 provides an overview. We begin by acknowledging the full complexities of the task by describing six barriers to be overcome.

Box 5.1: Challenges and opportunities

	Challenges		Opportunities
1.	The inhibiting grammar of schooling	1.	Building on a rich legacy
2.	The galloping centralisation of power	2.	Riding the wave of discontent
3.	Education alone cannot compensate for society	3.	The threats are intensifying
4.	Can the mainstream learn from the periphery?	4.	Powerful democratic professionals
5.	A history of repeated failure	5.	A model of change
6.	Wasteful and harmful competition	6.	First steps
		7.	Democracy as the way forward

The inhibiting grammar of schooling

As we argued in Chapter 3, the current, ramshackle 'system' has many weaknesses but it is resilient and durable: Seymour Sarason neatly captured this point in the brilliant title of his book, *The Predictable Failure of Educational Reform: Can we change before it's too late?*[6] The historical record is one of repeated, unsuccessful attempts to reform schools, where the schools have ended up absorbing or nullifying the reforms. Part of the difficulty is what David Tyack and Larry Cuban[7] called, in an arresting phrase, 'the basic grammar of schooling', by which they mean such organisational regularities as the division of knowledge into different subjects, the age grading of students and the private world of one teacher in a classroom with a group of students. These enduring features of our schools structure the taken-for-granted assumptions about education that we have all grown up with, but they also serve to stifle innovation. As a result, would-be reformers need a sophisticated understanding of schools, colleges and universities as social institutions, and of the professional culture of teachers, which varies from institution to institution and sector to sector.

We have no easy solutions about how to overcome the most disabling features of the present 'system'. We are sure, though, that reforms of the kind that are needed have to begin with a cool-headed, collegial and critical diagnosis of current practices. Unfortunately, this is not occurring within schools or workplaces to the degree that is needed. People grumble, of course they do, but our communities of discovery offer them effective ways to change their practice.

The galloping centralisation of power

The problem to overcome here is the growing impersonality and centralisation of power. Globalisation and turbo-capitalism have left national governments unable to control their economic and social policies. Such external forces have made governments all the more determined to exercise greater control over areas of domestic public life wherever they can.

Reformers in the UK would do well to consider Whitehall's centralisation of administrative power over education, which continues apace. Since 1960, through legislation, secretaries of state in England have acquired around 2,500 new powers. Despite all the rhetoric from the Coalition Government about returning power to the people, Michael Gove, the current Secretary of State for Education in England, is taking 50 additional powers in the Education Bill which is, at the time of writing in June 2011, being debated in Parliament. This is not creeping, but galloping, centralisation.

We need nothing less than a new settlement between central and local government and between these two levels of government and the teaching profession; a settlement that will distribute power more equally so that **democratic** local authorities take responsibility for educating all their children and adults, as well as acting as stewards of the public good by planning and funding education in a way that is fair to all.

The danger of further centralisation, however, is that the 'system' in England, which is already creaking, will fragment and may even collapse in some areas. How, for example, when all 25,000 schools have become academies or 'free' schools, which get their funding directly from the secretary of state, will he or she run the 'system'? We suspect that central government will then intensify its control over the schools and colleges that are directly funded by the state.

The obverse of this alarming growth in the power of ministers and civil servants is a serious waning of the power of professional educators. Teachers have been reduced to the role of technicians and agents of the state, whose job it is to 'deliver' a national curriculum devised by 'experts'; to make sure that the whole curriculum has been 'covered' in ways designated by the government; to be endlessly flexible; to be unthinkingly responsive to the government 'initiative of the week'; and to be permanently ready to be inspected. This accumulation of power at the centre has been replicated in schools, colleges and universities up and down the country, where a yawning gap has opened up between those who manage and those who teach; and where many, but by no means all, managers quietly put teaching to one side. Is it any wonder that so many teachers feel demoralised, when, as Dan Hind puts it, they have 'become conditioned to believe they are incapable of effective action, that achieving change is someone else's responsibility?'[8]

Education alone cannot compensate for society

Are our ideas sufficient on their own to ensure the radical changes we favour? Our answer is that they are not; they would have to work hand in glove with radical socio-economic and political reform.

Education cannot be expected to compensate for our grossly unequal society. Unless and until we have policies in place that tackle inequality in all its complexity and pervasiveness in the structures of this society, education will continue to reproduce it, rather than transforming it. The educational inequalities that we have highlighted are closely linked with inequalities in health, housing and employment; and they will not be reduced, never mind eradicated, until our educational proposals are part of a broader programme of social renewal, which requires action on the interrelated issues of increased minimum incomes; a fairer, more progressive tax system; and a vigorous industrial policy to create high-quality jobs. We need action on sub-standard housing on 'sink' estates; child and adult poverty; physical and mental illness; and crime, drug dependency and gang culture. And we need measures to prevent vested interests retaining their near monopoly of quality educational resources.

Richard Wilkinson and Kate Pickett summarise this argument well: 'Greater equality is the material foundation on which better social relations are built'.[9] We need a more just and sustainable economic model and a reformed structure of rewards more in keeping with social justice and social contribution than with personal greed or the supposed demands of the market.

Democratic renewal in education needs to be part of a wider programme of reform of our political institutions and processes; we need the simultaneous 'double democratisation' of both education and society, which Wilf Carr and Tony Hartnett called for.[10] Otherwise education will be helping to form active citizens who will only have a thin facade of democracy in which to live, learn and work. We need courage to take on change on this scale, but, as is being demonstrated daily in Arab countries, democracy is highly contagious. Studs Terkel remarked: 'Hope has never trickled down. It has always sprung up'.[11]

We are deafened by rhetoric from politicians from all parties about freedom and democracy, but we struggle to see any of the practice. The Speaker of the House of Commons, for example, prevented any discussion of Prince Andrew's use of public funds to represent this country's business interests abroad. We are not citizens. We are subjects under the Crown. The strength of democracy in education cannot be divorced from the strength of democracy in society more generally.

Can the mainstream learn from the periphery?

A further objection is likely to be that our plans are so idealistic that they may be enthusiastically introduced in the leafy suburbs, but would be quite impractical in downtown, deprived estates. Our reply is that many of the new methods of teaching and learning come precisely from those who have devised new ways of working with those who have achieved little or nothing inside the formal 'system'.

So ours is not an untried approach. Educators in our society who work with those who have been failed by formal education are working in this way all the time. In all phases and sectors, there are educators developing fresh ways to help people learn, and who have collaborated to find creative solutions to some of the most intractable problems of learning failure in our society. We can learn from their tried and tested experience.

In the world of those rejected by schooling there is exceptional work going on, as we discussed in Chapter 4. Those who work most effectively with this disengaged group – youth workers, work-based trainers, outdoor educators, staff working with young offenders – have discovered what it takes for such clients to re-engage with education. It starts with valuing them and respecting them; it requires their involvement; and the learning must have purpose and relevance to their lives. They have a right to be consulted.

Experiments in teaching and learning have been permitted at the periphery with pupils who are not as valued as those who are the success stories of mainstream schools. Does the mainstream, however, have the good sense to learn from these success stories at the periphery? We educators need to find the courage and initiative to look beyond our classrooms, schools and training rooms to learn from practice in other places.

A history of repeated failure

A further challenge is likely to come from those who know something of previous attempts to change educational systems. Why should our approach be any more successful than previous attempts? Such a question is likely to come from people with a strong interest in maintaining the status quo. The question also reflects an imperfect idea of civic engagement and an unwillingness to countenance fundamental change of those social institutions that generate the social inequalities, and the narrow, unachievable and materialistic aspirations that the economy depends on. To build democracy, we must live it. We need to acquire the habit of behaving democratically.

We have more chances of success, partly because we have tried to learn the lessons from earlier efforts, and partly because we want to introduce a new dimension which has not been tried before: namely, democracy. Seymour Sarason, whom we quoted above, criticised American reformers for choosing the wrong villains, just as our own politicians continue to do: teachers who are treated as 'inadequate', parents as 'irresponsible', and students as 'unaspiring'. Instead, he concluded that change will not occur unless the power relationships are altered significantly between those who are in charge of the 'system' and educators on the 'front line'.

Giving a greater role to educators in decision-making, however, is not sufficient for two reasons. First, educators cannot create and sustain the conditions for their students to become lifelong learners, if those conditions do not exist for the educators themselves; and those conditions currently do not exist in either the USA or the UK. This means in part transforming the initial and continuing 'training' of teachers from compliance with a list of over 100 'standards' into an education worthy of a profession. It also means our teachers acting as role models of active citizens for their pupils.

Second, Sarason argued that 'schools are uninteresting places in which the interests and questions of children have no relevance to what they are required to learn'.[12] In the 20 or so years since Sarason offered his reflections on reform, the working conditions of teachers have deteriorated and the curriculum has become overprescribed but unreformed, so the catalogue of repeated failure continues to lengthen.

Is it any wonder that the criticism of schooling most often heard from students is that it is 'boring'? We have learned from the work of many projects that young people reject formal education because too many of them find schools to be unsafe, threatening places in which they are shown little respect. Young people (with the exception of those excluded from school) are not sufficiently consulted about what they want to learn; they need to be engaged in a process of negotiating a curriculum that suits their needs. To be given choices from a pre-determined suite of course options is not the same thing. And it is little different in higher education. The 'choices' may be wider than in school, but for most students neither the content nor the manner of teaching, learning and assessment are negotiable. They are encouraged to act as consumers making choices, not as citizens shaping decisions about their academic lives.

Wasteful and harmful competition

We need a judicious balance between competition and cooperation, but under Conservative, New Labour and Coalition administrations, education has suffered from an excessive emphasis on competition. For example, parents, anxious about the lack of decent jobs, have been encouraged by government initiatives to act in the narrow self-interest of their children, which may make them **good parents**, but certainly makes them **bad citizens**, without a care for the deleterious effects of their selfish actions (in setting up 'free' schools, for example) on the education of other people's children. Policies which divert public funds disproportionately to the education of a few children undermine the spirit of community, and they strike at the heart of the cherished British value of fair play, hence the growing resistance to the initiative. Michael Young summed up our argument neatly when he wrote: 'Nearly all parents are going to try to gain unfair advantages for their offspring. The function of society…is to prevent such selfishness from doing any serious harm'.[13]

How, then, is it possible for educators to bring competition and cooperation into harmony with each other, when the continued existence of their institution is dependent on attracting students (and the funding attached to them) from rival organisations? The Coalition Government has chosen competition on a commercial basis as the main driving force for reform of all the public services. This is code for transferring public funds to the private sector. No sooner, however, has the Coalition Government praised to the skies the virtues of competition than it insists on the need for the very same institutions to collaborate, because its policies are heavily dependent on collaboration for their success. Nowhere do ministers explain, for instance, how it is possible for a comprehensive school to cooperate with a private provider that has been awarded the contract to undertake large swathes of work previously carried out by the school. Such commercial competition will exacerbate the already growing disparities between the educational attainments of the advantaged and the disadvantaged. In so doing, the market-led approaches now being pursued devalue the work of those educators who are dealing with the most challenging behaviour and from whom we all have much to learn. Besides, when a 'system' is already fragmenting, competition becomes positively harmful.

Opportunities

Each of the six challenges above presents a formidable obstacle, but together they constitute an interlocking set of barriers which help to explain why previous attempts at reform have only scratched the surface. Given the scale, complexity and intractability of these handicaps, we need to confront the possibility that communities of discovery are destined to become the latest in a long line of failed attempts at reform. We think not, because, in Raymond Williams' uplifting phrase, we shall call upon seven 'resources for a journey of hope'.[14]

Building on a rich legacy

The phrase above comes from a book, edited by Michael Apple and James Beane, which describes the long struggle to bring democracy to life in American schools: 'The efforts described here are not anomalies of our own times: they are contemporary examples of a long line of work that has stretched over more than a century'.[15] Those efforts include: the use of cooperative learning, not as a tactic to boost test scores, but as an essential feature of a democratic way of learning and living together; projects in Maryland, Wisconsin and California to connect the work of schools with local communities by studying serious local problems; and creating 'space in the curriculum for the study of large-scale social problems'.[16] Our communities of discovery are not, therefore, fantastical and impractical dreams – they are already living realities, which are today part and parcel of the daily experiences of some American students, experiences which draw on a noble tradition.

Similarly, there is a long, inspirational history of radical ideas in education in the UK, stretching back to the eighteenth and nineteenth centuries, to draw upon. Without it, the trades union and labour movement, the cooperative movement, the Workers' Educational Association, the Open University and the movement for the rights of women would not have developed. Each involved new learning, breaking with conventional thinking and taking radical action. These traditions have withered but they have not disappeared, as Michael Fielding and Peter Moss's new book makes clear.[17]

Inspiration can also be found in the innovative ideas of Loris Malaguzzi, who viewed the schools in Reggio Emilia in Italy primarily as sites for democratic and ethical practice. His notion of learning is listening to thought: 'the ideas and theories, questions and answers of children – treating thought seriously and with respect, struggling to make meaning from what is said, without preconceived ideas of what is correct or appropriate'.[18] Fleur Griffiths is working within this tradition in England through 'creative conversations'[19] with pre-school children, and producing wonder-full results that could easily be transferred to educating teenagers and adults.

Radical, democratic education has worked and is working successfully in practice. So our first resource is to set our proposals within a larger political, cultural and international history of the continuing struggle for democracy within education and society. We are not alone; we are part of a widespread movement whose time has come.

Riding the wave of discontent

For how long can the outdated, patched-up and overstretched juggernaut, which is our image of the current educational 'system', continue to run on, coughing and spluttering? With the huge, additional pressures being applied to it by the Coalition Government for it to move ever faster, in another (mistaken) direction, and fuelled with irrelevant ideas from the 1950s, the juggernaut is becoming an embarrassing and damaging anachronism. Further hectoring of teachers by government ministers to make this 'system' work more efficiently in the cause of improving the competitiveness of British industry is falling on deaf ears, because educators have, for over 20 years, heard and seen through their superficial message.

When either of us has given talks over the last few years, we have been taken aback by the depth and breadth of the discontent at the baleful effects of the overly rigorous testing regime on all those concerned. Parents are increasingly anxious about the repeated stress their children are subjected to every year from age 5 to 25. Teachers feel themselves being systematically de-skilled, de-professionalised and over-managed, as all the major decisions about what and how to teach are made by politicians and civil servants, who are dangerously remote from classrooms. Students have been drilled to pass tests, but even those with the highest grades report that they understand neither the subjects they have studied nor the major problems facing the world they have inherited.

The pressures from all these sources are growing: teachers in England have gone on strike because of proposed reductions to their pensions, and alliances have been forged between students of higher and further education to oppose cuts in Education Maintenance Allowances and the steep increase in university tuition fees. The student population is aware that the links between qualifications, jobs and income have been broken, and that the scramble for the declining number of professional/managerial jobs is worsening every year, so they are questioning the sacrifices they have made to become qualified but underemployed. When these pressures reach boiling point, as they are likely to do soon, people will start casting around for an alternative. Communities of discovery are our contribution to the public debate which should start now.

The threats are intensifying

In Chapter 2 we presented a list of the main threats to our collective well-being. Those threats, far from being addressed, are continuing to grow in intensity, and we give three examples here. As we complete writing this book in June 2011 comes news that greenhouse gas emissions increased by a record amount last year to the highest carbon output in history, putting hopes of restricting global warming to safe levels almost out of reach.

Meanwhile, the banking culture has not changed and so we could be threatened with another public bailout by the taxpayer, which could prove to be even more massive than the one that took place in 2008. We would also have expected the nuclear disaster at the Fukushima plant in Japan to have sparked a review (and a revision) of the UK's determination to continue with nuclear power. In contrast, the German government responded to widespread political protests by announcing a phased elimination of its nuclear power industry. In our list we raised 12 such threats and we will watch with interest to see if any of them are included in the Coalition's current review of the school curriculum.

We now understand why John Goodlad, the distinguished American educator, finds the phrase 'school reform' an abomination, as it sums up for him all that is wrong with current efforts: a linear model of inputs and outputs, prescribed by well-meaning outsiders, whose initiatives show just how out of touch they are with our present realities and future threats. Instead, he (and we agree) prefers the term 'renewal', by which he means 'an essential characteristic of a robust democracy...a comprehensive overhaul'[20] of the purposes, conditions, policies and practices of education and of the process of renewal itself. 'Problems or alternatives are discussed, decisions are made, actions are taken, consequences are evaluated and the cycle continues'.[21] That is another community of discovery already in action.

Powerful democratic professionals

In our view, such renewal is unlikely to come from the appointed leaders of our formal institutions – the vice-chancellors of universities, the principals of FE colleges or the heads of primary or secondary schools – because they have become, as a result of the education explosion, the managers of multi-million pound businesses. Their time is absorbed in responding to the latest round of government initiatives and changes in funding, in ensuring the survival and growth of their institution, and in the day-to-day running of huge, complex, social organisations. There never seems to be sufficient time to exercise their equally important role as public intellectuals, who have a responsibility to initiate, and to participate in, internal and public debates about the state of education. We need institutional leaders who realise that working with colleagues in classrooms to improve learning is more important than manipulating data to micro-manage their organisation from their corridor of power.

Renewal on the scale we envisage is more likely to come from below, when tutors in adult, community and prison education, and in our formal institutions, begin to demand more democratic practices. Such has been the pattern in the USA; witness the conclusion of Michael Apple and James Beane:

> In none of the cases [of democratic renewal in American schools] was the impetus generated from the 'top'. Instead, bottom-up movements – groups of teachers, the community, social activists, and so on – provided the driving force for change.[22]

Obviously not all our institutional leaders or tutors are alike, and some of the former are agitating for change, while some of the latter are apparently happy to carry out whatever instructions they receive. Renewal on the scale we envisage calls for alliances to be formed among all those who despair of the current 'system', alliances which pull together changes instigated from the top with those demanded from the bottom. It also means building alliances across boundaries, such as those between education and the worlds of work, local communities and like-minded people wherever they are to be found.

In our communities of discovery, educators and learners become experimenters, researchers, thinkers, pragmatists and joint developers of a new curriculum. The traditional roles of tutors have been to act both as mediators of a rich, inherited culture and as experts in teaching and learning, who link that culture to the interests and lives of their students. There are now, however, new roles for educators – building support for a different diagnosis of our time; engaging wider constituencies of opinion to demand changes to the curriculum which are commensurate with the threats we face; and working democratically with all interested parties to bring about whatever changes are collectively agreed upon. In these ways, through working collectively, they become powerful democratic professionals, where power is exercised solely in the interests of others.

We do not want to be interpreted as suggesting that our communities of discovery will always end in agreed decisions. Our experiences of implementing change in complex, social organisations is that there is likely to be a wide range of responses from professionals when change is introduced: from **enthusiasts**, who are happy to evaluate their own practice publicly; to the **superficial adopters**, who wait for hard evidence of improvement before they commit themselves fully; to the **unengaged**, who do not attend meetings or who do not contribute to the discussions if they do; to the **resisters**, who have seen it all before and are not prepared to try what they dismiss as the latest 'flavour of the month'.[23] Resisters may in fact be trying to protect their students from too much change, or change introduced too quickly or without sufficient planning, when the stakes are so high in terms of exam results. Some may be pointing to the lack of safeguards for learners during periods of massive change; and others may just be resisting. As Michael Fullan argues: 'Monitoring the process of change is just as important as measuring outcomes';[24] and there are widely available texts like his to help staff deal with the complex processes of change.

We want to add a final element, which is missing from current debates about change in education: democracy is a form of governance that enables people to reach negotiated compromises from their political disagreements and differences of interest. When we claim that communities of discovery are models of democratic practice, we do not wish to assert that they are free of conflict. Quite the opposite; there will be disagreements, often passionately articulated. Unlike political parties, communities of discovery do not live 'in the house of power'[25] but in the realm of ideas and innovative practice. They build their work on a conviction that the truth of a matter can be decided on the basis of open debate about appropriate evidence. When conflicts are intense and apparently irresolvable, there is always, in a democracy, the right of citizens to appeal to the wider court of public opinion.

These new roles call for a re-formation of the professional identity of educators towards what has come to be known in Australia, the USA and the UK as **democratic professionalism**.[26] Its core is an emphasis on cooperation between teachers and all the other partners in education – students, parents, and business and community leaders. Democratic professionals exercise wider responsibilities than simply being in charge of the education of groups of students, which include working with others to improve the institution they work in, the educational 'system' and their local community. Professional educators also have collective responsibilities – to contribute to the formation and evaluation of policy (both local and national), and to the initial and continuing education of new and experienced members of their profession.

The movement towards democratic professionalism has developed as a response within the teachers' unions to the disempowering role of **managerial professionalism**, with its preoccupation with control, accountability and effectiveness, which has had such a devastating impact on teachers' morale. The collective power of democratic professionals, working in concert for the benefit of their students and society, is just another way of describing our communities of discovery.

A model of change

All governments talk the language of change – of deep, lasting and transformational change – but rarely, if ever, do they discuss *how* that change is to be brought about, because they lack an explicit model. Instead, their programmes of reform tend to be a confusing amalgam of different, and often incompatible, initiatives, which, it is hoped, will magically act together to produce synergy and success. But, without argument, evidence or pilot studies, this is just wishful thinking. An alternative approach would be to choose one of the leading models of change, like Cynthia Coburn's.[27] She argued that national systems of education in search of renewal need to move beyond numbers, beyond counting minimal improvements in test scores or in percentages of qualifications obtained. Her close analysis of the huge research literature on educational change led her to propose four interrelated dimensions which she considered essential for success:

1. **depth**, which refers to the nature and quality of the proposed change; it must challenge teachers' beliefs about how students learn and, as a result, alter their classroom practices and patterns of interaction
2. **sustainability**, where resources, time and support continue to be allocated long after the initial enthusiasm has dissipated

3. **spread** of the key principles from classroom to classroom, school to school, school to community and workplaces; and back again in the opposite direction until the daily routines of educators are infused with fresh thinking
4. a **shift in ownership** of the change process away from politicians, policy-makers and managers to the educators who must introduce the reforms in such a way that the process becomes self-generating.

It may well be that our politicians are fully acquainted with such research but that they choose to ignore it because they would lose power if its recommendations were to be acted upon. But whether they are aware of it or not, our communities of discovery need a model of change which has depth, sustainability, spread of effect and a democratic shift in ownership towards educators.

First steps

> 'Some changes have to start now else there is no beginning for us.'
> Sheila Rowbotham[28]

On the one hand, it would be against the spirit of our proposals for us to offer at this late stage a completely worked-out programme of renewal. On the other hand, we wish to suggest three ideas to kick-start the process.

First, education at all levels and phases from age nothing to 90 should be free; it should be declared a right of citizenship. Scotland has decided to offer free university education to its citizens (as do Finland and Denmark, for example), a decision which will make it very difficult for the Coalition Government in England to persist in charging £9,000 per student per year – a policy which has been hastily introduced without planning, trialling, consultation or even thought. The 2011 White Paper on higher education (*Students at the Heart of the System*) invites consultation, but of a very guided kind. The anchor points of the new Coalition policies in this sector are clear: increased private sector involvement in higher education; students as consumers who will be given new powers to hold universities to account; a tripling of fees, which may deter participation by students from poor backgrounds despite the loans and grants available; and more 'diversity', which is code for intensifying the existing hierarchy among institutions. Elite universities will expand beyond their current limits to accommodate those with better A-level grades and there will be cheaper higher education offered by degree-awarding FE colleges that will concentrate on teaching, unsupported by research or well-equipped libraries. In sum, these proposals amount to a dangerous experiment which may well result in the closure of those universities that have made the greatest efforts to widen participation. The 'tadpole philosophy' (see Chapter 2) lives on.

Second, private schools should demonstrate in detail why they should be considered charities. If they cannot, their charitable status, and the tax advantages it confers, should be withdrawn. Over 50 years ago, James Mursell rightly pointed out:

> *If the schools of a democratic society do not exist for and work for the support and extension of democracy, then they are either socially useless or socially dangerous. At the best they will educate people who will go their way and earn their living indifferent to the obligations of citizenship in particular and of the democratic way of life in general.*[29]

Third, the policy process in England is not only flawed, it is breaking down. Within the space of one week in the middle of June 2011, the Coalition Government had to withdraw some of the central provisions of its plans to reform the National Health Service and to liberalise the sentencing policy of the Ministry of Justice; meanwhile, lecturers at Oxford University overwhelmingly passed a motion of no confidence in the Minister for Universities and Science. These reversals are the predictable outcome of overcentralisation, the empty rituals of consultation, continuous government intervention, and the treatment of policy as the personal fiefdom of ministers and senior civil servants. We need to remind government, in Robin Alexander's words, that 'a national education system belongs not to ministers and officials but to all of us'.[30]

If the undemocratic method of policy formation had been a success, then there might be something to be said for it, but the reverse is true. There is a lengthening list of government initiatives in education which have needed urgent revision within years of being launched: the national curriculum, National Vocational Qualifications, General National Vocational Qualifications, Curriculum 2000, Modern Apprenticeships, Learning Accounts, Standard Attainment Tests and now Diplomas.[31] The Department for Education is a non-learning organisation. To prevent further debacles, teachers' representatives – the unions – need to play a full and equal part in the formation, enactment and evaluation of policy, just as they do in other civilised societies.

Democracy as the way forward

When Karl Mannheim reviewed the position of youth in modern society in 1941, preoccupied as he was with the need to find a way out of the world's crisis that would be based on democratic principles and not those of laissez-faire capitalism, fascism or communism, he laid great stress on the need for democratic planning that would enable people to live in solidarity with one another. He imagined a society that nurtured in people a courageous independence of mind that would allow them to be constructively critical of their society and the wider world of which it was a part. His approach was not a plan, but an idea, and he said this of it:

> the task of an idea is exactly this: to mobilise the creative imagination for a new purpose. Once this is achieved, the details can be worked out through common experience. And for this common experience we have not to wait…we have to start here and now.[32]

We are in a much better position now than our parents and grandparents were when Mannheim produced his diagnosis of the times. We have a much more sophisticated understanding of learning and a greater knowledge of the social determinants of life chances. We have more powerful means of communicating knowledge, information and experiences than people of his day could have imagined possible. What still remains to be discovered, as it always will, is how best to use our creative imagination for a new purpose and how to summon up the courage to do so. We hope this book gives our fellow educators some support in developing their democratic practice.

There is a better future to be realised, but it is not going to be engineered by the guardians of the status quo. It will be realised, if it all, through the determined action of committed democrats, living their ideals in the places where they reside and work. If we fail, there are those who will exploit nationalism, racism and resentment towards the disadvantaged to impose authoritarian solutions to the growing crises that threaten us. The challenge before educators is to enable their students to live as citizens in an open society. There is too much at stake not to take the risks of doing so.

Final comments

The nub of our case is this: the education 'system' we have is not the one we need. The testing regime is damaging our young people; and the audit culture is driving out innovation and destroying our trust in educators. We argue for an education that is democratic, inclusive, lifelong and built to respond to an adequate **diagnosis of our time**. We look forward to people working together in what we have called communities of discovery so that we can understand better the threats we all face, develop better ways of dealing with them, and articulate with the confidence of free citizens the kind of future we want to live in.

We wish to add one final and vital ingredient to the mix. No major advance in the troubled history of British democracy has ever been won without a struggle. As Frederick Douglass, the African-American abolitionist, argued in 1857:

> *If there is no struggle there is no progress. Those who profess to favour freedom and yet deprecate agitation…want crops without plowing up the ground, they want rain without thunder and lightening… Power concedes nothing without a demand. It never did and it never will.*[33]

It is high time we raised our voices to demand education for democracy. This is the fight of our generation: we educators need to reclaim our professional freedom of thought and action; to introduce a curriculum that deals with the threats we face; and to renew both our educational 'system' and our society through democratic values and practices. We *can* and *must* do it.

Endnotes

1   Wilkinson and Pickett, 2009: 231.

2   Crowther and Martin, 2005: 213.

3   QCA, 1998.

4   See Coffield, 2009.

5   Hills, 2010: 4.

6   Sarason, 1990.

7   Tyack and Cuban, 1995.

8   Hind, 2010: 206.

9   Wilkinson and Pickett, 2009: 265.

10   Carr and Hartnett, 1996: 189.

11   Quoted by Klein, 2010.

12   Sarason, 1990: xiv.

13   Young, 1961: 30.

14   Williams, 1983: 243.

15   Apple and Beane, 1995: 19.

16   Beane and Apple, 1995: 20.

17   Fielding and Moss, 2011.

18   Moss, 2005: 25.

19   Griffiths, 2010.

20   Goodlad, 2008: 22.

21   Goodlad, 2008: 24.

22   Apple and Beane, 1995: 23.

23   Coffield, unpublished research report, 2011.

24   Fullan, 1991: 25.

25   Weber, 1970: 194.

26   See Sachs, 2001, for more information on activist professionals.

27   Coburn, 2003.

28   Quoted by Fielding and Moss, 2011: 148.

29   Quoted by Apple and Beane, 1995: 23.

30   Alexander, 2008: 27.

31   See Stanton, 2008, for further details. To this list of flawed government initiatives can be added: the University for Industry (UfI); the Open Tech; the Open College; Training and Enterprise Councils (TECs); Training Access Points (TAPs); Learning and Enterprise Councils (LECs); the Learning and Skills Council (LSC); and Training Credits.

32   Mannheim, 1950: 53.

33   See Blassingame, 1985: 204.

Postscript

Since we completed this book in June 2011, Britain has been shaken by two events: the phone hacking scandal by journalists at Rupert Murdoch's News International and the riots and looting which followed the police shooting to death a black man in Tottenham. Additionally, in Norway, a right-wing fanatic, pursuing his war against immigrants, especially Muslims, massacred over 70 young people.

We were shocked by these events, but we were not surprised. It came as no great revelation that the scandal-promoting, gutter press in the UK, with the supine indulgence of our politicians, has for years been destroying the private lives of individuals in the relentless pursuit of profit, although the extent (virtually on an industrial scale) of the technological invasion of their privacy was not known. Similarly, the presence in inner city housing estates of thousands upon thousands of young people who have no stake in this society, and who therefore have nothing to lose by engaging in serious criminal activity in order to acquire consumer goods, has been the repeated finding of social research for at least the last 40 years. The murders in Norway were shocking, but this well-organised and articulate killer espoused a racist language that appeals to people economically and politically marginalised by their own societies, who feel threatened by a new 'Other', no longer Jewish but Muslim.

Both UK topics are explicitly mentioned in our book – the systematic distortion of reality by the mass media and the continuing neglect of the bottom 30 per cent of the school population, generation after generation. These events, together with the wilful refusal of political leaders to control the excesses of the bankers who have wrecked the global economy, are symptomatic of a profound democratic deficit in western societies. The tired, old and ineffective rhetoric in Prime Minister Cameron's recent speech on the moral decline of the country that he applied to rioters and their families, could equally be aimed at the financial elites, those looters in suits, who run the City of London.

As in previous moral panics in the aftermath of riots in the 1970s and 1980s, the fundamental structural problems of our society are fleetingly acknowledged and then flatly ignored. At best, responses to them are short-term and inadequate, like garden centres in Liverpool. There is no credible **diagnosis of our time** in most of the post-riot political discussion, though the proposed national enquiry into urban unrest may yet be a vehicle to build a stronger analysis.

Our book highlights the radical need to invigorate democratic practice in all areas of public life. **Communities of discovery** are not only the way to re-engage people, especially the alienated young – they are the route to the new ideas we need to build a fairer society.

Our collective failure lies in part in the very intractability and interlocking nature of these problems, for which there are no simple solutions; another part is the sheer scale of the resources and commitment needed to make serious inroads into them. We predict that the private sector of the economy – the 'market' – will not produce the jobs and the training required by young people. We also predict that the Conservative-led Coalition Government will produce a revised national curriculum which will have little, if anything, to say about any of these events or problems which pose such serious threats to our democracy. The Government's tactical responses will be effective in the short-run in screwing down the dustbin lid, but our politicians and policy-makers have repeatedly shown themselves to be incapable of taking a long term, structural approach to such problems. They have shown a catastrophic failure of the democratic imagination to build new approaches and to involve citizens in public life. We hope our book encourages our readers to demand a response commensurate with the scale and nature of our problems. If we don't, and if **you** don't, who will?

References

Alexander, R. (2006) *Education as Dialogue: Moral and pedagogical choices for a runaway world*. Cambridge: Dialogos UK.

— (2008) 'Testaments to the power of 10'. *Times Educational Supplement*, 16 May, 27.

— (2010) (ed.) *Children, Their World, Their Education: Final report and recommendations of the Cambridge Primary Review*. London: Routledge.

Appiah, K.A. (2005) *The Ethics of Identity*. Princeton: Princeton University Press.

— (2010) *The Honor Code*. New York: W.W. Norton and Company.

Apple, M. (2000) *Official Knowledge: Democratic education in a conservative age*. London: Routledge.

Apple, M.W. and Beane, J.A. (1995) *Democratic Schools*. Virginia: Association for Supervision and Curriculum Development.

Ball, S.J. (2008) *The Education Debate*. Bristol: Policy Press.

Beane, J.A. and Apple, M.W. (1995) 'The Case for Democratic Schools'. In M.W. Apple and J.A. Beane (eds), *Democratic Schools*. Virginia: Association for Supervision and Curriculum Development.

Bentley, T. (1998) *Learning Beyond the Classroom: Education for a changing world*. London: Routledge.

Bernstein, B. (1996) *Pedagogy, Symbolic Control and Identity: Theory, research, critique*. London: Taylor and Francis.

Beveridge, W. (1942) *Report of the Inter-Departmental Committee on Social Insurance and Allied Services*. Cmnd 6404. London: HMSO.

Biesta, G. (2005) 'Against learning: Reclaiming a language for education in an age of learning'. *Nordisk Pedagogik*, 25, 54–66.

Biesta, G., Field, J., Hodkinson, P., MacLeod, F. and Goodson, I. (2011) *Improving Learning through the Lifecourse: Learning lives*. Abingdon: Routledge.

Blassingame, J.W. (1985) *The Frederick Douglass Papers*, Vol. 3. New Haven: Yale University Press.

Bowles, S. and Gintis, H. (1976) *Schooling in Capitalist America: Educational reform and the contradictions of economic life.* New York: Basic Books.

Brown, P., Lauder, H. and Ashton, D. (2011) *The Global Auction: The broken promises of education, jobs and incomes.* Oxford: Oxford University Press.

Carr, W. and Hartnett, A. (1996) *Education and the Struggle for Democracy: The politics of educational ideas.* Milton Keynes: Open University Press.

Carrington, V. (2008) '"I'm Dylan and I'm not going to say my last name": Some thoughts on childhood, text and new technologies'. *British Educational Research Journal,* 34(2), 151–66.

Castells, M. (1997) *The Power of Identity.* Oxford: Blackwell.

Centre for Longitudinal Studies (2007) *Disadvantaged Children up to a Year Behind by the Age of Three.* London: Institute of Education, University of London.

Chomsky, N. (2004) *Survival and Hegemony: America's quest for global dominance.* New York: Henry Holt.

Coburn, C.E. (2003) 'Rethinking scale: Moving beyond numbers to deep and lasting change'. *Educational Researcher,* 32(6), 3–12.

Coffield, F. (2009) *All You Ever Wanted to Know About Learning and Teaching But Were Too Cool to Ask.* London: Learning and Skills Network.

— (2010) *Yes, But What's Semmelweis Got to do With my Professional Development as a Tutor?* London: Learning and Skills Network.

— (forthcoming) *Let's Build Co-Construction Together.*

Coffield, F., Borrill, C. and Marshall, S. (1986) *Growing Up at the Margins: Young adults in the North East.* Milton Keynes: Open University Books.

Coffield, F., Edward, S., Finlay, I., Hodgson, A., Spours, K. and Steer, R. (2008) *Improving Learning, Skills and Inclusion: The impact of policy on post-compulsory education.* London: Routledge.

Collingwood, R.G. (1942) *The New Leviathan or Man, Society, Civilization and Barbarism.* Oxford: Clarendon Press.

Cowley, S. (2010) *Getting the Buggers to Behave.* London: Continuum.

Croft, J. (2011) *Profit-Making Free Schools: Unlocking the potential of England's proprietorial schools sector.* London: Adam Smith Research Trust, ASI (Research Ltd). Online. http://www.adamsmith.org (accessed 2 June 2011).

Crowther, J. and Martin, I. (2005) 'Learning Democracy and Activating Citizens: A role for universities'. In D. Wildemeersch, V. Stroobants and M. Bron Jr. (eds),

Active Citizenship and Multiple Identities in Europe. A learning outlook. Frankfurt am Main: Peter Lang.

Curtis, P. (2009) 'Schools accused of "hot housing" to get results'. *The Guardian,* 14 January, 4.

Democratic Life (2011) *Response to the National Curriculum Review Call for Evidence.* Online. http://www.democraticlife.org.uk (accessed 28 April 2011).

Department for Business, Innovation and Skills (DBIS) (2009) *Skills For Growth: The national skills strategy.* Cm 7641. London: The Stationery Office (TSO).

— (2011) *Students at the Heart of the System.* Cm 8122. London: TSO.

Department for Education and Skills (DfES) (2004) *Five Year Strategy for Children and Learners: Putting people at the heart of public services.* Cm 6272. London: TSO.

ESRC (2010) *Britain in 2010: Making tough choices.* London: Economic and Social Research Council.

Fielding, M., Bragg, S., Craig, J., Cunningham, I., Eraut, M., Gillinson, S., Horne, M., Robinson, C. and Thorp, J. (2005) *Factors Influencing The Transfer of Good Practice.* Research Brief No RB615. London: DfES.

Fielding, M. and Moss, P. (2011) *Radical Education and the Common School: A democratic alternative.* Abingdon: Routledge.

Fullan, M.G. (1991) *The New Meaning of Educational Change.* London: Cassell.

Fuller, A. and Unwin, L. (2003) 'Learning as apprentices in the contemporary UK workplace: Creating and managing expansive and restrictive participation'. *Journal of Education and Work,* 16(4).

Galbraith, J.K. (1992) *The Culture of Contentment.* London: Sinclair-Stevenson.

Goodlad, J.I. (2008) 'A Nonnegotiable Agenda'. In J.I. Goodlad, R. Soder and B. McDaniel (eds), *Education and the Making of a Democratic People.* Boulder: Paradigm.

Gove, M. (2011) Department for Education Press Release, 20 January.

Griffiths, F. (2010) *Supporting Children's Creativity through Music, Dance, Drama and Art: Creative conversations in the early years.* Oxford: Routledge.

Grossman, D.C., Lee, Wing On, and Kennedy, K.J. (2008) (eds) *Citizenship Curriculum in Asia and the Pacific.* Hong King: Springer.

Gutmann, A. and Thompson, D. (1996) *Democracy and Disagreement.* Cambridge, Mass.: Harvard University Press.

Halsey, A.H. (1986) *Change in British Society.* Oxford: Oxford University Press.

Hanks, W.F. (1991) 'Foreword'. In J. Lave and E. Wenger, *Situated Learning: Legitimate peripheral participation*. Cambridge: Cambridge University Press.

Hills, J. (2010) 'Equality of opportunity remains a distant ideal'. *The Guardian*, Society, 27 January, 4.

Hind, D. (2008) *The Threat to Reason*. London: Verso.

— (2010) *The Return of the Public*. London: Verso.

HM Government (2010) *The Coalition: Our programme for government*. London: The Cabinet Office.

IEA (2010) *International Report: Civic knowledge, attitudes and engagement among lower secondary school students in thirty-eight countries*. Amsterdam: International Association for the Evaluation of Educational Achievement (IEA).

Johnson, B. (2011) 'A world shaped by shared experience'. *The Observer*, 22 May.

Judt, T. (2010) *Ill Fares the Land: A treatise on our present discontents*. London: Penguin.

Klein, N. (2010) 'Rebranding America'. *The Guardian*, Saturday Review, 16 January, 2–4.

Kuhn, T.S. (1962) *The Structure of Scientific Revolutions*. Chicago: Chicago University Press.

Lave, J. and Wenger, E. (1991) *Situated Learning: Legitimate peripheral participation*. Cambridge: Cambridge University Press.

Lee, J. (2010) 'Qualifications boom pays off for billion-pound exam boards'. *Times Educational Supplement*, FE Focus, 26 March.

Mannheim, K. (1950) *Diagnosis of Our Time*. London: Routledge and Kegan Paul.

Mannheim, K. and Stewart, W.A.C. (1962) *An Introduction to the Sociology of Education*. London: Routledge and Kegan Paul.

McNally, S. and Vignoles, A. (2010) *Project 5. Literacy and numeracy skills*. London: London School of Economics, Centre for the Economics of Education. Online. http://cee.lse.ac.uk (accessed 2 June 2011).

Mills, C.W. (1963) *The Marxists*. Harmondsworth: Penguin.

Moss, P. (2005) 'Loris Malaguzzi, the town of Reggio Emilia and its schools'. *ReFocus Journal*, Summer, 1, 22–5.

Mulgan, G. and Salem, I. (2009) *Fixing the Future*. London: The Young Foundation.

National Equality Panel (2010) *The Anatomy of Economic Inequality in the UK. Case report 60*. London: London School of Economics and Government Equalities Office, Centre for Analysis of Social Exclusion. Online. http://www.equalities.gov.uk (accessed 9 August 2011).

Nussbaum, M.C. (2010) *Not For Profit: Why democracy needs the humanities*. Princeton: Princeton University Press.

Oakeshott, M. (2001) *The Voice of Liberal Learning*. Indianapolis: Liberty Fund.

Oates, T. (2010) *Could Do Better: Using international comparisons to refine the National Curriculum in England*. Cambridge: Cambridge Assessment.

— (2011) Letter in *The Guardian*, 17 June.

O'Hear, A. (1991) *Education and Democracy: Against the educational establishment*. London: Claridge Press.

Osler, A. and Starkey, H. (2006) 'Education for democratic citizenship'. *Research Papers in Education,* 21(4), 433–66.

Panel on Fair Access to the Professions (2009) *Unleashing Aspiration*. The Milburn Report. London: Cabinet Office.

Popper, K. (1976) *Unended Quest: An intellectual autobiography*. Glasgow: Fontana/Collins.

Qualifications and Curriculum Authority (QCA) (1998) *Education for Citizenship and the Teaching of Democracy in Schools*. The Crick Report. London: QCA/Department for Education and Employment.

Ravitch, D. (2010) 'Why I changed my mind about school reform'. *Wall Street Journal,* 9 March.

Rees, M. (2004) *Our Final Century: Will civilization survive the twenty-first century?* London: Arrow Books.

Sachs, J. (2001) 'Teacher professional identity: Competing discourses, competing outcomes'. *Journal of Educational Policy*, 16, 149–61.

Sarason, S.B. (1990) *The Predictable Failure of Educational Reform: Can we change course before it's too late?* San Fransisco: Jossey-Bass.

Schuller, T. and Watson, D. (2009) *Learning Through Life: Inquiry into the future of lifelong learning*. Leicester: NIACE.

Scott, T. and Cogan, J. (2008) 'Democracy at a Crossroads: Political tensions concerning educating for citizenship in the United States'. In D.C. Grosman, Wing On Lee and K.J. Kennedy (eds), *Citizenship Curriculum in Asia and the Pacific*. Hong Kong: Springer.

Seltzer, K. and Bentley, T. (1999) *The Creative Age: Knowledge as skills for the new economy.* London: Demos.

Sen, A. (2007) *Identity and Violence: The illusion of destiny.* London: Penguin Books.

— (2009) *The Idea of Justice.* London: Allen Lane/Penguin.

Sennett, R. (2008) *The Craftsman.* London: Allen Lane/Penguin.

Shepherd, J. (2011a) 'Record numbers seek help with A-level stress'. *The Guardian,* 21 May, 10.

— (2011b) 'Climate change education should be excluded from curriculum, says adviser', *The Guardian,* 12 June.

Stanton, G. (2008) *Learning Matters: Making the 14–19 reforms work for learners.* London: CfBT.

Tawney, R.H. (1964) *Equality.* London: Unwin Books.

Thompson, M. and Wiliam, D. (2007) 'Tight but loose: a conceptual framework for scaling up school reforms'. Paper presented at the American Educational Research Association, Chicago, 9–13 April.

Tomlinson, M. (2004) *14-19 Curriculum and Qualifications Reform: Final Report of the Working Group on 14-19 Reform.* London: DfES.

Tyack, D. and Cuban, L. (1995) *Tinkering Toward Utopia: A century of public school reform.* Cambridge, Mass.: Harvard University Press.

Unwin, L. and Fuller, A. (2003) *Expanding Learning in the Workplace.* Leicester: NIACE.

Weber, M. (1970) 'Class, Status and Party'. In H.H. Gerta and C.W. Mills (eds), *From Max Weber: Essays in Sociology.* London: Routledge.

Wenger, E.C. and Snyder, W.M. (2000) 'Communities of practice: The organizational frontier'. *Harvard Business Review,* January–February, 139–45.

White, J. (2010) *Much Improved: Should do even better.* Online. www.newvisionsforeducation.org.uk (accessed 4 May 2010).

Whitehead, A.N. (1962) *The Aims of Education.* London: Ernest Benn.

Wilkinson, R. and Pickett, K. (2009) *The Spirit Level: Why more equal societies almost always do better.* London: Allen Lane/Penguin.

Williams, R. (1965) *The Long Revolution.* London: Penguin Books.

— (1983) *Towards 2000.* London: Chatto and Windus.

Wolf, A. (2009) *An Adult Approach to Further Education*. London: Institute of Economic Affairs.

— (2011) *Review of Vocational Education*. London: Department for Education.

Wood, A.T. (2008) 'What is Renewal? Why now?' In J.I. Goodlad, R. Soder and B. McDaniel (eds), *Education and the Making of a Democratic People*. Boulder: Paradigm Publishers, 29–45.

Woodhead, C. (2009) 'Middle class pupils have better genes'. *The Guardian*, 11 May.

Young, M. (1961) *The Rise of the Meritocracy: 1870–2033*. Harmondsworth: Penguin.